Virtues of the Irish Saints

Virtues of the Irish Saints

Lessons in Faith,
Peace & Love

Gary McLoughlin

Hatherleigh Press, Ltd.
62545 State Highway 10, Hobart, NY 13788, USA
hatherleighpress.com

VIRTUES OF THE IRISH SAINTS

Library of Congress Cataloging-in-Publication Data
is available.
ISBN: 978-1-961293-42-7

Printed in the United States
The authorized representative in the EU for product safety and compliance is Catarina Astrom, Blästorpsvägen 14, 276 35 Borrby, Sweden. info@hatherleighpress.com
10 9 8 7 6 5 4 3 2 1

Contents

INTRODUCTION

CONSIDERING THE FUTURE IN THE PAST

ALMOST THIRTY years ago, my wife Judith and I set out on a journey. Emigrating to America from our home in County Armagh, Ireland, this marked the beginning of the greatest adventure of our lives. We were apprehensive, we were excited, we were a little unsure, but we knew God would go with us.

Everything about America seemed so new, so big, so grand, so fast-moving...and it was. The Troubles, as the conflict in Northern Ireland was called, had thankfully just ended, and so the economic growth that is so obviously apparent today had not yet taken place. Our homeland was quieter in comparison to America, older and more traditional, but being in our late twenties, we were ready for change. We were ready for all things new, ready for a higher gear.

Today, however, we have quite a different view. While we acknowledge how good America has been for us, we've also come to recognize that every life needs perspective and grounding. To move forward in the right direction, we sometimes have to consider what is behind us and what has shaped us into who we are. My wife and I had to leave Ireland behind in order to discover just how Irish we were. We have always embraced a Celtic outlook to our spirituality without really recognizing it, but living as sojourners is what taught us to truly embrace the pathways of our past in order to discover the destinations of our future.

Each of us is on a journey in this life, a journey that is different for each person. Some people find an amazingly straight and easy road through life, one with few twists and turns, and are left to wonder what the fuss is all about, whilst others are on a proverbial rollercoaster of circumstances that can go off the rails unexpectedly. A job that seemed secure is suddenly gone with a market downturn. A relationship, once warm and fulfilling, has turned cold and painful. An untimely diagnosis, one that promises years of challenging recovery. Difficult circumstances, often not of our own making, and seemingly unfair. Life just has a way of dealing each of us a different set of cards.

Despite these factors, people insist on muddling through life at breakneck speed without considering alternatives. There is always somewhere to be, always something to do, and seldom do people stop to think about deeper things until they're forced to. We coast until we crash, and then and only then do we look for help. Pain and disappointment are surefire ways of stopping most people in their tracks, and when they do, they're bound to search for a different path. But sometimes, you need a friend on the road to point you in that new direction.

Life in twenty-first century Western society is beset with endless choices and convoluted complexity, but it wasn't always this way. Perhaps, it wasn't even *meant* to be this way. There was a time in the distant past when people thought more deeply about their life and the world around them, about the lives of their friends and family, about the journey and the sojourner, about the ethereal world of the hereafter, and what on Earth it all means.

If we took the time today to consider some of these people and the positive aspects of human experience they represent, what new knowledge could we glean? Why did they think as they did? What did they pursue with their relentless prayers and pilgrimages?

In the green hills of Ireland, a thousand or so years ago, such a time as this existed, a time that saw saintly people in spades. They lived out an ancient Celtic spirituality and took exhaustive amounts of time over the course of their entire lives to consider the questions we inwardly ask today, but don't consider pursuing because we are simply too busy and distracted. What if we could stop for just a moment and consider the lives these people lived and what they achieved? What lessons could they teach us today?

What does it mean to have a Celtic outlook on life, and do we have anything to learn from looking back toward the past in order to sort out some of our future? What ancient Celtic virtues might we discover to help direct our own journey?

THE COMFORTING GREEN SHORE

Today, millions of people visit Ireland for a variety of reasons, but when distilled to its essence, they come in search of natural beauty, historical curiosities, and a warm culture that embraces the stranger as friend—a culture that remains true to its very ancient roots in terms of faith, language, music, sports, and the arts. There is just something healing about the land and the Irish culture.

Over many years of bringing people to Ireland on tour, we've found visitors' reactions to this island nation have a few things in common. Visitors are amazed that Irish people are willing to stop and hold conversations while being earnestly curious about the other person. The speed of life somehow seems slow enough to catch your breath for a moment, as you take time to feel the breeze off the wide Atlantic. Small towns and villages evoke a sense of community that is stubbornly non-commercial yet somehow deeply rooted. Pubs without wall-to-wall TV screens; cafes without a sea of laptops; deep conversations. The scale of it all seems a bit more human, somehow. Small green fields with stone walls that also seem a bit more manageable. Mountains that can be hiked in just a few hours and see you back in the pub for a pint before dark. The deep green everywhere, a constant comfort as you navigate the winding roads between the hedgerows.

And through it all, the evidence of history that seems to be everywhere. Standing stones; old, ruined castles; long-abandoned stone houses; these reminders dot the landscape and sit strangely idle in fields surrounded by milling cattle. Ridges line the base of mountains, showcasing evidence of potato cultivation in even the most remote and seemingly inhospitable places. At just a glance, you can tell that people have lived on this island for a very long time, and with that longevity comes the lived experience over an age that shapes a culture.

This is the old Celtic spirituality which imbues the land with its slow and steady rhythm, a beat which most are unconsciously aware of and are attracted to, but find hard to describe. The rhythm speaks of ancient virtues that are different and curiously strange, but which we can perhaps unpack a little through the stories of lives lived long ago.

STANDING STONES, LEGIONS AND SAINTS

The very ancient people that lived in Ireland many millennia ago left few clues to their culture and language, save the strange stone monuments and ring forts found on many hilltops, especially along the eastern coast. Newgrange in County Meath might be the most famous with its huge entrance stones and intricate spiral carvings that invoke a trinity. Illuminated each year on the Winter Solstice for reasons that escape us, but which point to the sacred. Standing stone circles which pose more questions than answers, but all hint at a people who looked up instead of down, who sought answers and pursued the ethereal. In County Armagh, our home county, archaeologists discovered evidence of a huge and intricate wooden fort that was constructed on a hilltop at a sacred place called Navan, then ritually burned to the ground. No one really knows why, but the mystery alone is intriguing enough.

Then came the Celts (also called the Gaels) with their language and swirling art forms and clan life based in community. They dominated these ancient islands on

Europe's western fringe and thrived in the dark oak forests and cold misty mountains that so intimidated the Romans. While the Caesars waged and won their many battles and almost obliterated native Gaelic culture throughout Northern Europe two thousand years ago, the Irish Gaels survived the Roman onslaught isolated on their island. Here, they continued with their closeknit communities, speaking their wonderfully lyrical Gaelic language as they named the rivers, mountains, and glens around them in their native tongue, names which still survive today.

The Roman Empire transformed the rest of the European continent into a culture modeled after its own, one which would eventually lead to the Western world as we know it. But as they looked across the gray Irish Sea, the Romans beheld the strange island to the west of Britannia which they nicknamed "Hibernia," the land of constant winter. Too cold a house for these sophisticated Mediterranean dwellers, they left it mostly alone, and thus the precious Gaelic culture survived.

Of course, many more struggles would happen on this island in the centuries that would follow, but the important point is that Gaelic culture survived in Ireland where it did not in the rest of mainland Europe. This is highly significant, as we will come to see, as the coming of Christianity to the island created a cultural and sacred hybrid of faith and community, one which was wholly unique: a truly *Celtic spirituality.*

A SACRED REVOLUTION

As the Roman legions began retreating back to the Italian peninsula in the early fifth century, and in the midst of the collapse of the Western Empire, Christian teaching made an entrance into Hibernia. This "invasion of faith" would be much more successful than any legion or Caesar could have dreamed.

Christianity was already present in Ireland, having been imported from Britain and Gaul through slaves and trade, but it was not organized. After what appears to be a failed attempt at organization by a Gaulish deacon called Palladius in 431 AD, Saint Patrick arrived in 432 AD at a place now called Saul in County Down. This would set in motion an epic evolution of the peoples of these islands, one that still reverberates to this day. This sacred revolution would eventually engulf and transform an entire nation and culture, in time spawning many more legends and saints that continue to teach and inspire us, and who ultimately led me to write this book many centuries later.

I'm sure these wonderful saints would be quite amazed at all this attention. To them, they simply followed the faithful path of hope and love, despite the difficulty of the world they were born into.

As you turn the pages of this book, my hope is to introduce you to some of these Irish saints and their Celtic spiritual culture. I hope their stories of faith, struggle, and love inspire you to perhaps see your own circumstances with a new perspective. Celtic spirituality, as it would eventually be known, has become very precious to myself and my family as we navigate the competitive world of the 21st century. Sometimes, it is good to step back and reflect on the current era with an eye and an ear to the beauty and poetry of the sacred past.

Celtic Spirituality

Finally, if I may, let me complete this introduction with some clarifications and thoughts on the meaning of the term "Celtic Spirituality."

Over the last 30 years, there has been an exceptional interest in and revival of Celtic Spirituality. In the course of the stories told in this book, I'll be referring to this term many times. So, you might ask, what does it really mean?

Honestly, I do feel the terminology has been a bit overused, which has led to a dilution of its meaning.

For many people, it might mean some sort of New Age mysticism or environmental awareness, or else a trendy cultural awakening. It can mean all those things, and many embrace differing aspects of being Celtic in terms of music or dress or what have you.

But for me, and for context here in this book, Celtic Spirituality will simply refer to the particular Christian faith culture of the British and Irish Isles of the first millennium and beyond. The Christian Celtic spirituality taught by these wonderful Irish saints embraces community, everyday rhythms, and poetry; it finds the sacred in the mundane, and sees the Triune God everywhere. They loved and lived to the fullest. They prayed and sought the face of God in a brutal time. They embraced humility and rejected class distinctions. They embraced the world through the lens of the existing bardic Gaelic culture of those Western Isles, as it was at that time, and so their Christian faith became a hybrid of sorts. They spoke Gaelic languages but also spoke and wrote in Latin, and they left us a heritage to follow—a Celtic, Christian heritage.

For almost seven hundred years, the Celtic Christian spiritual tradition flourished in Ireland and Britain, influencing and guiding the cultures of emerging Europe until it was finally merged into the more established Roman church in the Middle Ages. King John, himself no friend of Ireland, forbade Irishmen from becoming bishops within the church in 1216. And so, with neither influence nor leadership, the Celtic sacred way simply melted into history. But perhaps, through the pages of this little book, I may prompt your interest in this precious heritage.

So, walk with me, if you will, along this ancient Celtic path. Let's discover some of these incredible characters and saints from the sacred green island we call Ireland, drawn from a time very different from our own.

Joy in the journey!

Saint Patrick

Courage

BEING IRISH in America affords at least a few privileges, such as a strange accent, freckled skin that burns with the slightest glimmer of summer sunshine, and a knack for sarcasm (albeit one that is lost on most people).

However, there is one undeniable perk. Every year on March 17th, we get to claim our very own American holiday: namely, Saint Patrick's Day. A day where the country turns green, parades light up cities and towns, and a lot of fun is had by all in the tackiest of green sweaters. Amazingly, though, the majority of people aren't even aware of the namesake behind the green-tinged shenanigans. Most are quite content to revel in the vague Irishness of it all, but Patrick was very much a real person—an actual man whose life is surprisingly well documented for the time he lived in.

THE SAINT AND THE HOLIDAY

Patrick was an inspired yet faithful man whose life was and is an ongoing inspiration to millions. However, if you are fairly new to the legend of Saint Patrick, there are some essential facts about him that might surprise you. If you look beyond the snakes and the shamrocks, you'll find a humble soul who lived with admirable candor and perseverance, despite impossible odds.

To begin with, Patrick wasn't Irish. Gaelic was not his native tongue and Irish culture was entirely foreign to him. But God has a way of taking the most improbable people from seemingly impossible positions and placing them in the most unexpected places, and so it was with our groundbreaking patron saint.

Patrick lived in the early fifth century, itself a turning point in history both for the early Christian church and for the world in general. The great empire of Rome, which had dominated the Mediterranean world and the continent of Europe for eleven centuries, was imploding. An established world order and a way of life that had thus far stood the test of time was vanishing, and in the span of one lifetime would be swept away almost completely. This stoic and oppressive empire with its rules and regulations and order of things would retreat, replaced by what historians call "*The Dark Ages*," a time of chaos and feudalism that would halt progress in many aspects of society and culture—a complete reset of the status quo.

Patrick was born a Roman Briton, growing up in this established way of life, but by the time of his death on the 17th of March 461 AD, the world was turning a corner. No longer would there be a common language or system of government, no set of traditions or class system in common, no single monetary system, and so on. Into this world came a man who would make a difference, a man of great courage and insight.

FROM ROMAN CAPTIVE TO IRISH SLAVE

We know many of the details of Patrick's life through two of his letters that have survived through the centuries. These are his "Confession," which is essentially a sacred biography; and a second letter to a brutal British chieftain named Coroticus, who seems to have been guilty of preying upon Patrick's Irish flock, with Patrick's views on the matter made pretty clear. The survival of these writings is very rare for a person from this point in history, offering us a valuable glimpse into his life in the fifth century.

Born sometime in the closing years of the fourth century to a Roman landowning family, Patrick grew up in a village called Bannaventaberniae in what is now northern England. At the time, however, this area marked the very edge of the Roman Empire in the province of Britannia. The Emperor Claudius had finally captured most of the island of Britain in the first century, overwhelming its Celtic British tribes, and had established a very settled province, one that would see relative peace for centuries. To keep this peace, the

Romans built a huge wall across its northern border, dividing what is now Scotland from England to keep the Pictish people at bay. They also strove to keep the Irish Gaels across the cold sea at arm's length. Both were viewed by the Romans as horrific Barbarians, and as such were left to their own devices.

Patrick's father, named Calpornius, was a decurion, similar to a town councilor, and as such they were members of the "*Patrician*" class, as opposed to the Plebeian class of Roman society—itself a tantalizing clue into the name by which this young man will eventually be called. His family was nominally Christian, but this comfortable life would suffer great upset when a raid by Irish pirates on his village and the surrounding area swept Patrick into captivity.

Slavery was commonplace at this point in history, with most slaves captured in petty wars or raids such as this to be used as commodities for farming and menial work. A fit, young boy like Patrick would be very useful in such a slave economy, and so he was captured and ferried across the Irish Sea to Ireland and a new life of mundane work in harsh circumstances.

It is difficult to pin a definitive timeline or geographical location to his slavery, but many believe he began his captivity in the northern province of Ulster. Then, through slave sales and trades, he wound up somewhere in County Mayo in the west of Ireland. Here, we know from Patrick's own words that his last owner kept him working on the rough mountainsides for six years. It would seem to make sense that he began his captivity in Ulster and ended it in Mayo, as along the way he picked up both the languages and the customs of these distinct Irish regions, all of which would prove incredibly valuable in his later life. His intimate knowledge of both Ulster Gaelic and Western Gaelic allowed him to navigate their distinct cultures and customs.

It is always a source of inspiration to me when I discover that the backstory of one of my heroes involves years of preparation and turmoil which they later put to such good use. Virtually no one who lives a life of significance, as Patrick did, arrives at that place easily.

As a slave boy, young Patrick likely spent a lot of time tending animals and sheep on high hills and exposed mountainsides where the thick oak forests weren't as encroaching. Life there would have been very harsh indeed.

Growing up in the North of Ireland in Armagh and Down, it is somewhat easier for me to imagine how difficult life would have been for a young boy on the cold, wet mountain slopes of Ireland. I hiked the Mourne Mountains in County Down many times as a young man, and had to constantly take shelter behind stone walls as the wind and rain lashed the landscape and chilled you to the bone. Consider for a moment how difficult life would have been for a young man from a comfortable setting to be thrust into such a landscape. Abused by owners who spoke strange languages, wore strange clothes, ate strange foods, and did not value your life at all. No doubt violence was used as a tool of subjugation as well.

But despite this, Patrick would find the strength to climb out of this dark valley, and it all began with prayer.

PRAYER, HOPE, ESCAPE AND RESTORATION

One of the factors of Patrick's life at this point would have been long periods of solitary existence. Alone on the mountain, surrounded by livestock, Patrick rekindled the faith of his fathers and began to pray and cry out for salvation. Patrick cried out for years, persisting in the pursuit of God until he received a very direct answer in the form of a vivid dream.

In this vision, he heard a voice say to him, "*Look, your ship is ready*," and in the morning that followed, he somehow found the courage to embrace this message of hope. There and then, he began to lay his plans of escape, despite his bleak circumstances. No doubt he knew well the consequences for runaway slaves—violence and probable death—but escape he did. He chose his moment and ran from his captor of six years, running east into the unknown heartland of Ireland. He progressed by taking advantage of a network of other sympathetic Christian captives scattered throughout the country, fellow slaves and countrymen who were working the land. These brave souls would have given him shelter and direction as he crossed the fields, bogs, and dark oak forests, heading for an unknown shore.

In time, he made it through without capture and stumbled across a waiting ship as he reached the eastern shoreline, just as God had revealed to him in the dream, showing admirable courage for one so young in such incredible circumstances to set out for freedom.

Perhaps this shows us that taking a leap of faith in such circumstances is a good investment. If God says it, it will happen. Perhaps in ways we did not anticipate, but will happen nonetheless.

And so Patrick found his promised ship, against all odds, but the trials did not end there. The pagan captain of the ship wasn't exactly welcoming of a runaway slave who had no means of payment and whose very presence could jeopardize his crew. Yet miraculously and through desperate prayer, Patrick was able to board. He settled in with the crew and they sailed away from Ireland across the Irish Sea and landed several days later, making port in either Britain or Gaul.

So far, so good, you may say. But at this point, the story takes a strange direction. Patrick describes wandering in what he calls a "*desertum,*" or wasteland, for 28 days to the point of starvation. At this time of peril, his hapless crewmates reacted to their plight with a cynical eye. 'How could this happen?' they asked. 'Surely the Christian God you follow should save you, no?' All seemed lost, but true to form, Patrick prayed. And, to the utter amazement of the pagan crew, they miraculously stumbled across a herd of pigs which they could exploit for food. Yet another miracle born out of prayer and faith, a good fit for Patrick's overall common narrative and one with interesting parallels to Biblical tales of want and miracle provision.

To modern readers, this story may seem a bit strange. After all, if you step off a boat anywhere on the western English or French coast today, you couldn't get 100 yards before finding a fence, or at least a road or a petrol station. But in the early fifth century, most of Britain was uninhabited rough land and forest. Imagine the Yorkshire moors without Heathcliff or Cathy or anyone for a hundred miles!

Eventually, Patrick would find his way back to his village in what is now Northern England, where he rebooted his life. He picked up the pieces and began a healing process that would take years, one in which he decided to place faith at the center of all things. No doubt kindled by his miraculous escape, he cultivated a persistent faith that would continue to burn bright in his heart for the rest of his life.

In time, he became a priest in the church, and over the next 15 or so years he would embark on a deep spiritual dive, making up for the lost years and lack of formal education that he was denied due to his capture and enslavement. Interestingly, these lost years and lack of schooling as a boy would be a wound for Patrick that would mark him throughout his ministry. At his own confession, he was embarrassed by his poor grammar and vulgar Latin, but he nonetheless pressed on and pursued education and sacred training. God was preparing him.

Think of how much easier it would have been to lie low and live a quiet life after such upheaval and turmoil. It is an inspiration to me that he did not rest on his laurels, but instead pursued education and purpose—and thank God he did!

VICTORIUS AND THE CALL OF THE IRISH

One night, after many years of study, Patrick's life would take another sharp turn. He had yet another vision in his sleep. This time, however, the dream had the opposite effect of the first one he had received back on that blustery hillside in Ireland. In this dream, a character called on him to go back to Ireland, returning to all that which he had tried to put behind him. In the vision, he saw a figure whom he called "*Victorius*" who came to him with sackloads of letters from the Irish. He took one, and in his own words, it read: "*We ask you, holy boy, come and walk once more among us.*"

Patrick was cut to the heart and did what for most of us would be unthinkable. He decided to return to the pagan land where he had known only persecution, estrangement, and violence. He heard the voice calling him back, knew it for the voice of God, and he answered the call—Ireland's call.

The mentality required for such a decision is so without regard for oneself that it must be God-inspired. Who among us would choose a difficult and dangerous path when living in relative security, particularly when we have suffered grievances previously from the same source?

The question is, why did Patrick turn and redirect his life so abruptly? A clue can be found in the manner of Patrick's writings. It is evident that Patrick was a humble soul, very dependent on the protection of the Trinity, which he would later evoke in his famous prayer. Here was not a man known for pursuing his own self-interests but rather one who followed a calling. Was all this a shot in the dark? I believe it was a great mission, one that went against all common sense and urges of self-preservation, but Patrick chose to believe God and ignore his own fears.

It might be interesting to ponder for a moment the fact that, if not for this return to Ireland, we would likely never have heard of Patrick. He would have melted into the ether of other well-meaning Christian clerics of the era, a lucky escapee with an interesting story. Faithful, but forgotten. But this was not to be so for Patrick, as his fate took a different course.

Patrick *did* return to Ireland, landing at Saul near Downpatrick in Ulster, setting in motion a movement of faith and culture greater than he could have ever dreamed of. In time, he would set up many fledgling church communities and would preach to kings and chieftains in exalted places such as Tara in Meath and Ard Macha in what would become Armagh, the ecclesiastical capital of Ireland. Twin cathedrals, both named Saint Patrick's, now stand on hills where the great man preached.

Thousands would experience freedom through the life of one humble but courageous man, and we would see a land of saints and scholars arise to bless the nations, punching far above its size and population. The success of Patrick's mission in Ireland is truly the stuff of legend. Yes, he was strategic, and yes, he was certainly clever in his arguments, but it is incredibly difficult to lead a sacred revolution without some key ingredients.

CALLING AND COURAGE

Firstly, I believe Patrick was called to a very specific purpose, just as we see in the Biblical account of Moses, another reluctant and other-centered person who was called to a particular mission. Moses upended the world's leading military superpower of his day, itself led by a demigod; clearly, God was with him. Patrick's writings do not paint a picture of a particularly forceful or arrogant person, but of someone filled with self-doubt. In fact, just as Moses may have struggled with his speech, Patrick may also have stammered, which made his preaching exploits all the more miraculous.

He was not an elite; he was not particularly polished. He just humbly obeyed, and God did the rest.

Secondly, and this is what I reflect on often, Patrick had enormous courage. It took incredible guts to follow this mission, despite the nature of his calling. He may not have been a General Patton-type, blindly charging the hill; he just took a courageous single step in faith, then another, and another, all in the same direction. Small steps, taken in the same direction, not knowing the outcome, but taken with courage. Trusting God to do the heavy lifting—which He did.

So, the question is, do we have the courage to take those small steps? Perhaps we aren't called to immediately change enormous things, but only small issues. Small steps—yet, when measured over a lifetime, small, faithful steps in the same direction can lead to significant change.

Patrick may not have known great fame in his lifetime. He certainly wasn't wealthy, and in fact may have been without any possessions. He didn't take a wife or rise to any great political office. He lived the rest of his days in Ireland, the land to which he was called, faithfully and humbly serving the people around him. No doubt he would be amazed to know that we are discussing his life centuries later. But he had courage, and that courage endured, changing the world for the better.

Perhaps we could find a small grain of such courage and change someone's world, and in doing so, change our own for the better.

The Prayer of Saint Patrick

Many are the stories of Patrick's life and mission, some of which are no doubt legend, such as those famed tales of shamrocks and snakes, but his determination is clear. His vision was far-reaching, his humility exemplary, and his dependence on God total. All of these traits are visible in his words and his famous prayer:

I arise today
Through the strength of heaven;
Light of the sun, Splendor of fire,
Speed of lightning, Swiftness of the wind,
Depth of the sea, Stability of the earth,
Firmness of the rock.
I arise today
Through God's strength to pilot me;
God's might to uphold me,
God's wisdom to guide me,
God's eye to look before me,
God's ear to hear me,
God's word to speak for me,
God's hand to guard me,
God's way to lie before me,

God's shield to protect me,
God's hosts to save me
From snares of the devil,
From temptations of vices,
From every one who desires me ill,
Afar and a-near, Alone or in a multitude.
Christ with me, Christ before me, Christ
behind me,
Christ in me, Christ beneath me, Christ above me,
Christ on my right, Christ on my left,
Christ when I lie down, Christ when I sit down,
Christ in the heart of every man who thinks of me,
Christ in the mouth of every man who speaks
of me,
Christ in the eye that sees me,
Christ in the ear that hears me.
I arise today.

Saint Brigid

Generosity

IN 2022, Ireland instituted a new public holiday for the first time in a generation, setting aside February 1st to be celebrated as Saint Brigid's Day. Irish people now officially take a day off to enjoy family time together or dig in the garden in preparation for spring planting, all in honor of the patroness of Ireland, Saint Brigid.

Truthfully, though, the body politic was only catching up with the reality that Irish people have lived with for years. Brigid is a longstanding, ongoing and important inspiration to millions. Children learn to make Saint Brigid's crosses in school, with their four distinct arms woven from reeds; farmers hang Saint Brigid's crosses in milking sheds and parlors seeking protection for their animals; and parades and rituals happen in towns and villages, just as they have for centuries—all in her honor.

A WORLDWIDE INSPIRATION

Brigid is celebrated in Ireland, that is for sure, with many women of Irish descent bearing her name in its various spellings and forms, but she is also honored and celebrated throughout the world, often without people knowing it. Location names using Bree, Bride, and Bridie, such as can be found in the Scottish Isles, all honor Brigid. Medieval knights, when choosing their young noble virgins for marriage, would give them the title of 'bride' in honor of their patron saint, a name that stuck. Today, millions of women wear white and walk the isle as brides, unknowingly honoring a very kind and generous woman who lived in Ireland fifteen centuries ago.

But who was Saint Brigid? And why do so many people, past and present, find inspiration in her life? What can we learn from Brigid's words and deeds all those years ago? And what ancient Celtic Christian virtues did she display that we might learn from?

THE THREE PATRON SAINTS

Along with Saint Patrick and Colmcille, Saint Brigid fills out a trinity of patron saints of Ireland. Interestingly, all three are rumored to be buried in the same grave plot in Downpatrick in County Down, as the famous rhyme says:

"In Down three saints one grave do fill:
Patrick, Brigid and Colmcille."

We will walk through her story and legacy together, learning her importance in the story of Celtic Spirituality. But before we talk about her life, we need to address one particularly large elephant in the saintly room—and that is the current scholarly trend that teaches that Saint Brigid wasn't even a real person at all.

Could that be true?

A Pagan Goddess of Fire, Hearth and Healing

The feast day of Saint Brigid falls on February 1st, which also just happens to be the ancient pagan feast day to mark the festival of *Imbolc*, one of four ancient Celtic festivals based on the seasonal calendar that have been celebrated in Gaelic lands for millennia.

Those would be:

- ***Imbolc***, February 1st: Marks the beginning of spring and the advent of lighter days.
- ***Bealtaine***, May 1st: Celebrates the start of summer.
- ***Lughnasadh***, August 1st: Celebrates the beginning of the harvest or autumn season.
- ***Samhain***, November 1st: Celebrates the end of the harvest and the onset of darker winter days ahead.

Today, Samhain is the most famous, as it became the festival of Halloween in Ireland during the Christian era, now celebrated on October 31st. This was in turn imported into American culture by Irish immigrants. Once in the USA, it took on a complete life of its own with its pumpkin spice lattes, ghost stories and trick-or-treaters.

It is significant, though, that Saint Brigid's day coincides with the festival of Imbolc, as it just so happens that the pagan Celtic goddess celebrated at Imbolc—the goddess of fire, hearth, healing and poetry—was also named Brigid.

The name '*Brigid*' means 'exalted one,' and this pagan goddess was certainly important to the ancient Celtic people of Ireland. It is said that she "*brought the spring*" and initiated the beginning of lighter days in the year which, if you have ever endured a long, dark Irish winter, can be a very welcome sight, indeed.

Could it be that Saint Brigid was not a real person at all, then, but instead a Christian invention? Simply the imposition of a personality on top of an already-existing pagan goddess? If so, that's some smart marketing on the part of those wily early Irish evangelists. Could Irish monks, writing of Brigid's exploits a century later, have fabricated the entire story?

Of course, this line of thinking is not unique to Saint Brigid or even to Ireland. Many have long insisted that several ancient Christian figures are simply repackaged, previously existing pagan sources. The story of Noah's Ark may actually be a Mesopotamian legend; the dark figure of Satan may have Zoroastrian roots, and so on. This is a well-worn path, but my personal belief is that whilst Brigid does share many aspects with her supposed pagan forerunner, I still believe she was a real person, born in the right place at the right time for a purpose.

The truth is that many ancient figures are shrouded in mystery. In the case of Saint Brigid, her story was not written down for at least a hundred years after her passing, so it is possible that some creative license was used by the monks who lovingly wrote about her whilst also being steeped in Gaelic folklore and story as they were.

However, the many details of her life do point to a real person, such as the minor tribe she apparently belonged to, the geography of her life, the locations of her monasteries, and so on. If you were going to make up a story, you might be tempted to place her closer to the centers of power than she was or give her a much more noble lineage than she had. So, whilst the Irish love a good story, the many aspects of her life don't need to be discarded completely. No need to throw the baby out with the proverbial saintly bath water; instead, we can find great inspiration in the life of Saint Brigid of Kildare.

And so we shall.

In our modern, information-driven world with its need for multiple sources of verification, we may find it strange and perhaps disingenuous that Christian writers would use their imaginations to fill out a story. Does this make it a false narrative? I say no—it was merely a way to tie together separate strands of truth to make a whole. It was story-telling!

So, who exactly was Saint Brigid?

A DAUGHTER BORN OF A KING AND A SLAVE

Despite some wishful thinking that claims Saint Brigid was a disciple of Saint Patrick, this was probably not the case (although their lives did overlap by a decade or so). Saint Brigid was born around the year 450 AD in Faughart, in what is now County Louth on the eastern coast of Ireland, as part of the second generation of Irish Christians that came after Patrick's missions.

The circumstances of Brigid's birth are quite unusual. She was born the daughter of a pagan Gaelic chieftain whilst her mother was a slave called Broicsech (Brocessa). The story goes that her mother, much like Patrick, was a captive of Irish raiders—caught in the northern Iberian Peninsula and brought to Ireland to be sold into servile bondage. Brocessa eventually ended up in the service of the pagan king Dubhthact (Duffy) of Leinster, and eventually became pregnant with the king's child. As one might imagine, the king's wife wasn't overly happy about this pregnancy, and so King Dubhthact was pressured into selling Brocessa to a druid (a pagan priest) in the north of his kingdom. It was there that Brocessa gave birth to Brigid. Brocessa and her daughter served the druid together for most of Brigid's childhood.

Brocessa, Saint Brigid's mother, was a Christian and it is clear that she instilled in her young daughter the morality and tenets of the Christian faith at an early age as they worked together as slaves. Brigid began her life walking the road of the lowly, never forgetting her roots and life of humble service, which goes some way to explain the humility and care for the needy that Saint Brigid exhibited throughout her life.

Even though Brocessa was a slave, the king did have some affection for her. After his queen lost a baby of their own, the king brought Brigid back into his household and raised her as his daughter. King Dubhthact named

Brigid after the Celtic goddess of fire and hearth, as we have previously explored, and this naming alone indicates a level of honor. Names in ancient times were always significant, and naming this baby girl after such an important Celtic goddess speaks of the importance of her birth and the affection the king felt for her. It was a title of honor, not to be taken lightly.

Many of us also have difficult backgrounds with split family situations or poor upbringings. Should we harbor bitterness from this legacy or use it as a springboard to identify and help others, as Brigid did?

After Brigid had gone to live in the king's household, the druid who owned Brocessa took her to Connaught in the west of Ireland, leaving Brigid alone in the service of the king. Even in her mother's absence, Brigid grew in faith and character and appears to have held a clear devotion to God with a compassion for the people around her, particularly those of low estate. She gave away practically everything she had to others, and as a slave, she encountered people in need daily.

Her father, however, was not so pleased by this exuberant behavior from his daughter. Yes, she remained a slave, but she also had the privilege of royal lineage. Eventually, it seems her Christian ethics and generosity became too much of an embarrassment. When he could take it no more, Dubhthact arranged to sell her to his overlord: the High King of Leinster, Dunlang MacEnda.

However, God had other plans.

The High King was a Christian, reportedly baptized by Saint Patrick himself decades earlier, and the trade did not go exactly as planned. Dubhthact took Brigid with him in his fine chariot to negotiate her price with the High King, but as the girl waited in the chariot, a poor leper happened along the road and asked for charity from the royal household. Taking great pity on the man in need, Brigid longed to help him. It was then that she spied the Dubhthact's jeweled sword, one of his most prized possessions, sitting there in the chariot.

The sword was of great value, a gift from MacEnda himself, which Dubhthact no doubt brought along to impress the High King. Yet without a second thought, Brigid pulled the sword and gave it to the poor man to his great and utter surprise. Sometime later, when Dubhthact realized what Brigid had done, he flew into a rage in the presence of the High King, furious at Brigid's unabated generosity.

As I mentioned before, the High King was a

Christian and was duly impressed by the piety, generosity, and poise of this young woman. As the young Brigid was dragged before the High King, he asked her if she would give away *his* wealth just as easily. Brigid, with clear honesty, answered that she would give away all the wealth of the kingdom to the poor and needy if it were hers to give. Astonished by this reply, the High King declared that Brigid's status was higher in God's eyes than any in his kingdom and, turning to his throne, pulled his own jeweled sword from its scabbard and presented it to Dubhthact as compensation, declaring Brigid to be of immense value—certainly of more value than any sword. She was not to be sold that day.

Have you ever been tempted to give in to popular opinion or felt pressure to conform to the cultural norms? Doing the right thing might cost us reputation and societal advantage, but in God's economy, doing what is right will always be honored…eventually.

Stunned by this turn of events, father and daughter returned home. In time, Dubhthact recognized Brigid's special and unique character and granted her freedom.

The king attempted to find a husband for Brigid, but she turned away from such offers. She felt she had a clear calling from God. Instead of marriage, she did something groundbreaking for that time period, something that would reverberate throughout the ages. With great courage, she left the king's household and gathered seven other young women who shared her passion to embark on a journey to create a community of faith for those who wanted to serve the poor, educate the ignorant, and serve the community. For women to embark on such a task was certainly counter-cultural for the fifth century!

It must be said that Gaelic culture within Ireland in the fifth century did offer women an astonishing degree of freedom and dignity when compared to other cultures around the world at that time. But still, this action by Brigid would see the lives of countless women changed for centuries to come.

The women led by Saint Brigid sought out the care of Bishop Mel in Ardagh, another early Christian leader from that second generation after Patrick. Bishop Mel consecrated these seven friends and conferred upon Brigid an Episcopal order, essentially making her a bishop herself in the service of God. It is said they dressed in white robes, which was at the time the garb of pagan druids, and countless stories of their miraculous dealings and provisions abound from this time as these young women began to make history. They set about creating a settlement for themselves nearby at Croghan Hill in the Irish midlands: Ireland's first monastic center in Kildare.

Kildare, today a thriving suburban hub with golf clubs and horse farms not far from Dublin City, means "cell of the oak" (Cill-dare) and is the place where Brigid and her sisters founded Ireland's first Christian monastery. Oak trees were sacred to Celtic pagans, with druids performing many rites under oaken groves, so it only made sense to build the monastery somewhere that was *already* sacred to the local people. They changed the sacred place to one where people received mercy instead of condemnation, charity instead of judgement, peace instead of war mongering, and love instead of enmity.

One of the miracles attributed to Saint Brigid happened during the founding of the monastery at Kildare. It is said that she asked the king of Leinster for land to found the monastery, and he declared she could have as much land as her cloak could cover—which seems, on the face of it, to have been a cruel and sarcastic joke.

> The ancient Irish people wore a cloak called a "mantle" which was so tightly woven it was waterproof, and was such a distinctive part of Gaelic dress that the English overlords banned the wearing of mantles in the 17th century.

To the king's great surprise, she removed her cloak and rolled it out, and it rolled and rolled and rolled until it covered the entire Curragh of Kildare! This miracle is a testament to the faith of Brigid, who had no means or resources other than her faith, and of God's beneficence and His willingness to provide for those He loves.

WOMEN IN CELTIC CULTURE

In time, people would learn of the fame of Saint Brigid's Kildare and of the many stories of mercy and miracles that were taking place there. Saint Brigid converted and baptized thousands as she carried on Patrick's legacy, creating a haven for the poor. Her generous heart extended deep into the Irish culture. No one was turned away. Through her love for others and her acts of lavish generosity towards those who could never repay her, she earned a place in the legacy and fabric of Ireland itself. Not bad for an illegitimate slave girl born into bondage!

This legacy very much confirms the positive and accepting role that women played in the early Celtic church, which in turn ran through an early Celtic culture that saw women as leaders, priests and teachers. This is admirable and certainly sets it apart from its early Roman neighbor, which carried a male-dominated hierarchy from its Mediterranean and Roman cultural roots.

Brigid was a leader and an inspiration, as much then as now, but sadly the role of women was somewhat diminished after the Council of Whitby and its subsequent effects on the Celtic church. The Council of Whitby was an early medieval council where Roman spirituality was chosen over Celtic spirituality (see the later chapter on Saint Aidan). A black mark on our history, but through Brigid's inspiration, we can turn this around. The flame of Brigid's generosity still burns bright today, challenging us to leverage her story in our lives. Are there women in our churches and groups who might have been overlooked, but perhaps deserve a more prominent role?

In a world that promotes greed, do we have the heart to give to those in need without expecting return? What jeweled sword would we give away in service to others?

A Prayer Inspired by the Life of Saint Brigid

Let me finish with an ancient and traditional prayer to Saint Brigid that has been used in Ireland for a long time, which speaks of this extraordinary woman of simple faith who loved others more than her life and set in train a movement that still holds sway today.

Brigid, you were a woman of peace.
You brought harmony where there was conflict.
You brought light to the darkness.
You brought hope to the downcast.

May the mantle of your peace cover those who are troubled and anxious.
And may peace be firmly rooted in our hearts and in our world.

Inspire us to act justly and to reverence all God has made.
Brigid, you were a voice for the wounded and the weary.

Lord, strengthen what is weak within us.
Calm us into a quietness that heals and listens.
May we grow each day into greater wholeness in mind, body and spirit.

Amen.

Saint Colmcille (Columba)

Peace

SEVERAL YEARS ago, my wife and I were traveling and working in Scotland and decided to make a pilgrimage of sorts to the sacred Isle of Iona, off the western coast of Scotland in the Inner Hebrides. The small island of Iona is the resting place of Saint Colmcille (also called Columba) along with no less than 60 kings of old. It was also the site of a great center of learning and inspiration founded by Saint Colmcille in the sixth century.

Like many Christians in Ireland and Scotland, we knew about the wonders of Iona and how the light of Europe was rekindled from there in the Dark Ages. We'd heard about the wonderful illuminated manuscripts written there and the terrible Viking raids it endured. It had captured my imagination for many years. How on earth could this remote little rock on the edge of the world host such a monumental place in history? We had to see it for ourselves.

Traveling to Iona is not for the casual traveler or day tripper. The island is situated off the coast of another island, located off the rugged coast of western Scotland. It requires two ferry crossings and many hours of driving on remote, single-track roads, and while the scenery is quite breathtaking, the journey can be taxing. Coming from the Scottish mainland, we left the port of Oban and crossed the Sound of Mull to Craignure on the Isle of Mull, then traveled west to Fionnphort, a small village at the very tip of Mull. From there, we took one more short ferry ride.

As we boarded the small CalMac ferry, we decided to go to the top deck and look across to the island as the boat pushed out from the slip. It was a fine evening, the sun was shining, and the sea breezes were exhilarating as we began the short crossing, looking toward the island as we went. Just then, a single wild goose coming from the north swept in across the water in front of the boat. It skimmed the waves, circled around the ferry, and flew off across the sea. My wife Judith and I looked at each other in disbelief, mouths open and wide-eyed at what we had just experienced.

For those of you who may not be familiar with Celtic symbolism, the Wild Goose was a symbol for the Holy Spirit within the early Celtic church, and remains so today. As such, Judith and I were sure that we had just witnessed a *theophany*—a visible manifestation of the divine.

THE SACRED ISLE AND THE WILD GOOSE

For us, crossing to Iona was the pinnacle of a journey into Celtic Spirituality that had stretched back to our youth. As we looked at each other in disbelief, we knew that we were on the right path. We were thirsty for more, we were hungry for God, and as we looked back to Iona with great joy in our hearts, we thought of Colmcille and his friends as they made this same journey 15 centuries ago: looking for God, searching for truth, and hoping the Wild Goose would go with them.

The question is, why did the saint choose such a lonely and remote place off the coast of Scotland when he could have chosen a more comfortable path, even reigned as a king in Ireland? Clearly, Saint Colmcille encountered several crossroads along his way that directed him in unexpected ways. Life in general and the hand of God have a way of doing that. Perhaps we can learn from his eventful ancient path.

Always a subject of fascination for me is how we as humans shake our fists at the sky and blame God for calamity and the unexpected detours in our life. But when we look back with hindsight, we see that the route, though it seemed strange and uncomfortable for us, was planned by God all along.

THE PRINCE AND THE DOVE

Known across the world as Saint Columba but known in Ireland as *Colmcille*, this great leader of men was an inspiration to thousands in his lifetime and to millions today. Born in Gartan, County Donegal in 521 AD, almost one hundred years after Saint Patrick, he is probably the most revered Irish-born saint—one whose life took many twists and turns before he crossed the Irish Sea and landed on that lonely beach at Iona.

Baptized as "Crimthain," which means "fox," he soon acquired the nickname "Colum Cille," which means "dove of the church" in Gaelic. This name was derived from his early devotion to the faith and his frequent attendance at the small chapel where he grew up. The nickname stuck, and in later years he was referred to as "Columba," which is the Latin form of the name. (*I may upset some of my Irish readers here, but for ease of understanding, I will refer to the saint as "Columba" from this point on.*)

Columba was of high noble birth in his native home of Ulster, the northern province of Ireland. The great-great-grandson of Niall of the Nine Hostages, he was a prince of the O'Donnells, a branch of the royal *Ui Neill* clan (O'Neill). In fact, had his life not taken the turn towards the sacred that it did, he could have been a strong chieftain, perhaps even the High King of Ireland given his distinct leadership and negotiation skills. He was, however, called to lead men to peace, not to war, though not before overcoming a few missteps along the way.

Interesting to consider how history would have been different had Columba taken the most direct route in his life and claimed kingship in Ireland. Yes, he would have led a significant life, but also one of little impact. In following his sacred calling and establishing the Iona community, he provided a route out of the Dark Ages in Europe. Proof that our decisions matter!

Young Columba was a fine student, and accounts from the time all depict him as a tall and handsome man who would affect all around him. He trained as both a prince, one who learned the art of war and poetry in the Gaelic tradition, while also devoting himself to sacred studies in the land of the O'Neills. The young prince was tutored by Finnian of Movilla and by the bard Gemman, eventually earning a place as a student with Saint Finnian of Clonard, the most influential teacher of his day.

Learning from Saint Finnian was an honor, and Columba spent many years under his mentorship, claiming for himself a place among the famed "*12 Apostles of Ireland.*"

During these years of sacred intensity, Columba proved himself a natural leader by helping to found several monastic sites of learning and study, the most significant of which is Derry in the northwest of Ireland, a thriving city of culture today. He also had a hand in establishing Durrow, Swords, Kilglass, and Drumcliff in Sligo, where W.B. Yeats is buried. Columba was a busy monk indeed, and his influence was significant in his native Ireland. However, before his story was finished, a certain event transpired—one that would go on to redefine and redirect Columba from his path and which is revered as a turning point in western Ireland.

That event is known as "The Battle of the Book."

THE BATTLE OF THE BOOK

Accounts of Columba suggest that he was a bit of a polymath, with several polished skill sets. He was a leader, a poet, a priest, a great orator, and on top of all this, he had great skill in scripting. Scripting is the skill of writing sacred texts, and in this period of Irish history, scriptology was emerging as a phenomenon that even today fills all those who observe the sacred texts with wonder. Examples of these sacred texts are the Book of Armagh, the Book of Durrow, and the famed Book of Kells, which was written on Iona. The sheer beauty of these manuscripts is breathtaking, and I would strongly encourage my readers to pay a visit to Trinity College in Dublin to see the Book of Kells in person.

During his many years with Saint Finnian, Columba was able to study a precious book of the Psalms that had been brought to their monastery from a pilgrimage to Rome years earlier. In the sixth century, and in a remote corner of the world such as Ireland occupied, such a book would have been precious beyond measure—a thing of wonder. Columba not only had access to this precious book, but he also decided to discreetly make a copy of his own. Working in secret over many months, Columba snuck into the scriptorium and, word for word, made a copy on vellum of the precious psalter.

It may seem trivial to us today that a student would make a copy of his master's book, but in the days of the first millennium, copying such a treasure was a very big deal. So much so that when Finnian, the Abbott, discovered what Columba had been doing, he objected in the strongest terms and demanded to have Columba's copy back. However, Columba refused to relinquish it. This led to a quarrel between the two great men that was so unresolvable that it had to be adjudicated by the highest authority in the land.

King Diarmait (Dermott) was the ruling High King of Ireland in those days and no friend to the O'Donnells, Columba's clan. He was duly asked to make a ruling on the matter, which essentially involved a judgment on copyright, possibly the world's first ruling on copyright infringement. Did Columba, by his efforts and ingenuity, have a claim over the new book? Or did rights revert back to Finnian, the owner of the original? In Gaelic society, it was common for the chieftains to make all sorts of rulings on disputes, and in the end, King Diarmait, who may have had a bone to pick with the O'Donnells, ruled against Columba and ordered the book to go back to its original owner, uttering the now famous phrase: "*To every cow belongs its calf, and to every book its copy.*"

This ruling was, of course, a huge blow to Columba, who returned empty-handed to his native clan in Ulster, chastised by this rebuke. The O'Donnells had been insulted.

As if this wasn't enough, another event happened which proved to antagonize the situation. Prince Curnan, a close relative of Columba's, had accidentally killed a high-ranking contestant at the Gaelic games at Tara in King Diarmait's realm. Because of this death, Prince Curnan fled, taking sanctuary with Saint Columba in his monastery back in Ulster. In response, King Diarmait's soldiers pursued Curnan, captured him within the monastery grounds, and brought him back to Tara, where he was tried and executed for his alleged crime.

The violation of the sanctuary of Columba and the death of Curnan, along with the book ruling, was just too much to take. And so Columba and the O'Donnells took up arms against King Diarmait. They each raised armies amongst their respective kinsmen and fought a great battle near the modern town of Sligo, where it is said that 3,000 men died in violent combat—a conflict which resulted in defeat for King Diarmait.

EXILE, REMORSE AND RECONCILIATION

The aftermath of this battle had profound implications for Columba. He was a renowned man of the cloth who had taken up arms and as a result, he was summoned before a synod of the ecclesiastical body. Columba was almost excommunicated for his part in the insurrection; however, Saint Brendan of Birr came to his defense at the last moment. Rising from his seat, he approached Columba and kissed him on the cheek in an act of mercy and forgiveness. Because of this act of mercy, the council relented and refrained from applying the ultimate sentence. Instead of excommunication, Columba would be allowed to go into exile whilst retaining his position as a priest and monk.

Columba was certainly scarred by the experience, and he withdrew to seek penance and solitude on Devinish Island in Lough Erne, in County Fermanagh. It must also be said that Columba appeared to suffer great remorse over the deaths caused by the battle and was resolved to put things right as best he could. He decided to turn away from politics and the strife so ever-present in early Gaelic society. He resolved to reconcile both his own conscience with what he knew to be true and to reconcile with his fellow Gaels. Clearly, he saw, violence and retribution were not the answers. But what is?

How do we deal with remorse and guilt when faced with truth in the light of day? Do we recoil and nurture our woundedness, or can we use grace as a springboard to reconciliation?

Over the next few years, Columba gathered twelve friends, and together in search of peace and penance, they left their beloved Ireland to go to the Hebridean Isles. At the time, the area of Argyll and the Western Isles off the coast of Scotland were part of the Dal Riada Kingdom, ruled from what is now County Antrim in Northern Ireland. The people of the region were kinsmen and spoke the same Gaelic language. It is also claimed that the island Iona was gifted to Columba by the King of Dal Riada, who was a kinsman of Columba.

Columba and the twelve arrived on Iona around the year 563 AD and set about building a church and shelters for communal living. This would be a new page for Columba. No doubt they struggled in those early years, but Columba's fame and renown drew more pilgrims and brothers to the tiny island, which resulted in the development of an active Christian community. This community would grow to be the spark that rekindled the flame of Christianity.

The isle of Iona today is a prominent place of pilgrimage within the British Isles. A tiny island that sits within beautiful turquoise waters with pristine beaches, it attracts many thousands of pilgrims each year who are seeking God, or a place of solace. Sometimes, we all need a 'place' of rest, of sabbath—somewhere we can see life in perspective.

THE EDGE OF THE WORLD BECOMES THE CENTER

Over the next few years, decades and indeed centuries, Iona developed into the very epicenter of Celtic Christianity. It spawned many great works and saints that had profound influences on the world as it struggled with feudalism and darkness following the collapse of the Roman Empire. It may seem odd to us today that a remote island off the Scottish coast could be the center of anything; however, we must remember that at this time in history and throughout the early Medieval era, it was much more convenient and efficient to travel by sea compared to land. Iona was perfectly and strategically placed to travel far and wide throughout the British Isles, Ireland, Europe, and Scandinavia, when making similar journeys over land would have been impossible. There *were* no roads. Thick forests and bogs covered the land and mountains, making even the shortest journeys hazardous.

And so this island, itself only three miles wide, was located on the equivalent of a super-highway. It also established itself as a hub of sacred activity which evangelized and educated not only Scotland but also Europe over the next few centuries. Columba is reported to have scripted three hundred books himself, and hundreds of sacred texts copied and written on Iona made their way throughout the world in a time when the art of writing had almost disappeared. The famous Book of Kells was created on Iona around the year 800, during the island's golden age, and was smuggled to inland Ireland to keep it safe from Norse raiders. Today, the book stands as a testimony to the skill, artistry, and faithfulness of those who toiled and lived on Iona following in the footsteps of Saint Columba.

It is believed that many illuminated manuscripts were created during this Celtic golden age. However, most were lost in the last three centuries of the first millennium to Viking raiders whose apparent interest was only the gold and bejeweled covers, not the pages of the books themselves, which were discarded and lost.

FROM WAR, PEACE

In hindsight, it seems that God used the Battle of the Book and its aftermath as a springboard to build something greater—something profound that would reverberate through the centuries and lead to peace as the result of war. All things really do work for the good of those who love Him. Even today, the Iona Community is a worldwide ecumenical Christian group that strives for peace and justice in the world.

My wife and I could sense that peace as we walked the paths of the sacred isle, surrounded by aqua blue waters, its beaches beautiful and tranquil. Columba's remorse from the Battle of the Book, and the determination to seek justice and peace, rings loud even today.

Columba traveled throughout Scotland and ministered to the Pictish people outside of Dalriada, making peace wherever he went. It is even said that he befriended and converted King Brude, the pagan king of the Picts, and was able to broker a treaty between Brude and King Cormac that created long-lasting peace between the Gaelic and the Pictish people. The dove of the church had lived up to his childhood nickname and became the inspiration for peace, even for myself growing up in Northern Ireland during a time of war and conflict.

Even though Columba participated in violence and strife, he turned his life around for the sake of peace. Drawing inspiration from that, we can, too. Perhaps you haven't led an army into a battle, but you may have made misjudgments in your life that you regret. If so, may the life of Columba be an inspiration to you. Your story has not yet ended, and may you also find peace and justice on your path as Columba did.

The Prayer of Saint Columba

I will end Columba's eventful tale with a simple prayer dedicated to the man, written in the Celtic style. It is simple yet profound, and reflects the man who once led an army into battle but later realized that simplicity and peace are the higher roads.

O Christ, King of the Bright Heaven,
Guardian of the wandering soul,
Fold us now in Thy mantle of peace,
And still the restless waves within.
Where swords have clashed, let mercy bloom,
Where words have wounded, let kindness heal,
Where fear has darkened, let hope arise,
And where hatred lingers, let Thy grace abide.
O High King of the Sacred Isle,
Make us vessels of Thy holy peace,
That we may walk as pilgrims of light,
And bear Thy blessing to the world.

Continued on the next page

By the strength of the Trinity,
By the wisdom of the saints,
By the love of the angels above,
Let peace be ours this day and evermore.
Be thou a bright flame before me,
Be thou a guiding star above me,
Be thou a smooth path below me,
Be thou a kindly shepherd behind me,
Today, tonight and forever.

Amen.

Saint Brendan

Adventure

HERE IN the United States, we have a national holiday called Columbus Day. Although the day is now mired in some controversy, it does nevertheless mark the discovery of the Americas by Europeans, which helped initiate the modern era.

As significant as Columbus's landing was, the glaring problem with the American discovery narrative lies in the fact that people were already living in the Americas when Columbus stumbled across the Caribbean islands. In fact, not only was the area already inhabited—many sophisticated cultures existed throughout the continent and its many islands, civilizations that could have competed with European cultures on multiple levels. Yet the old saying is true: "*History belongs to the victors.*"

But did you know that there are tales and legends of earlier explorations from Europe to the Americas, ones that pre-date Christopher Columbus? The tale of Saint Brendan just happens to be one of them.

SAILING THE OCEAN BLUE

Several years ago, my wife and I were in Mexico and took a trip to an ancient Maya city in the Yucatan Peninsula. It was startling, mysterious, and impressive with its pyramids rising out of the rain forest in their silent vigil. The people who lived here were clearly not brute savages as the European explorers reported; these were cities that illustrated a culture of wonderful art, architecture, and engineering.

The whole experience started me thinking about the Spanish conquest of the Aztec people, and how crazy it really was. It just seems so improbable that the Spanish adventurer Cortés could get the better of the Aztec King Montezuma, but somehow he did.

Embedded in the story of Cortés and Montezuma is a tantalizing clue to the history of foreign explorers in this part of the world. Montezuma treated Cortès as a returning folk hero or demigod. As the story goes, it was almost as if Montezuma was *waiting* for the return of this pale figure, who had become part of the Aztec religion and folklore. Now, this might refer to many things, such as existing gods of their time, but some also argue that this folklore might hide a nugget of truth: that pale-skinned Europeans visited this continent before in the distant past, a story that passed into legend.

Might they have? Did a saint called Brendan really discover the Americas and sail to many other places in the northern hemisphere, following his calling as a missionary pilgrim?

In my study at home, we have a relief piece of art on the wall, a reproduction of an ancient stone carving from Ireland. It's called the "*Bantry Boat*" and it illustrates four sailors in a *currach*, an ancient Irish boat, rowing heavenward while a fifth figure holds the rudder and guides the boat from the stern. The original carving is on the Kilnaruane stone pillar in County Cork, erected there in the eighth century at a site believed to have been a monastery founded by none other than Saint Brendan. Some have suggested this strange carving of sailors in the currach might be allegorical in some way; the sailors and the boat depicted on the stone pillar are placed vertically, after all, rowing their way to heaven. But the easiest explanation is that these mysterious sailors represent the story of *Saint Brendan the Navigator*, as he would come to be known, and celebrate his fantastical voyage to the island of paradise.

Brendan's story is as intriguing and mysterious as it is inspiring. As we live our lives of routine with traffic, schedules, school lunches, football practice, client meetings, and endless bills, it can be refreshing to let our thoughts drift to ones of adventure. We all love stories of daring and exploration, and for good reason—I believe we were made for more than the mundane. Perhaps we were made to wander, explore, and discover the vastness of God and his creation. After all, the atmosphere above us is amazingly thin and transparent, allowing us to see the expanse of the universe at night when it could have easily been translucent, as astronomers have noted on other planets. We look at the stars and they drive us to wonder. They entice us to discover mysteries, and perhaps the life of this ancient Irish wanderer has a few well-worn paths for our journey to consider.

What does adventure look like in your life, and how did it look to Saint Brendan? Why did he risk it all on the open seas and travel to the ends of the Earth?

Let's find out.

A KERRYMAN, HE WAS

Although most of the records we have about Brendan were written at least one hundred years after his death, we can be sure that he was born around 484 AD in what is now County Kerry, near the town of Tralee on the southwest coast of Ireland. So, Brendan is what we in Ireland call a Kerryman!

(Even though I am a Northerner, I have to confess here that Kerry is one of my favorite places in Ireland—with its beautiful and rugged coastline, picturesque mountains, and quaint villages.)

Legend tells us the names of Brendan's parents were Finnlug and Cara, while he was born with the name Mobhi. However, at his baptism he was given the nickname "*Broen-finn*," (Brendan) which means "*fair drop*," due to his appearance. As we have seen with other Irish saints from this era, the name stuck.

His birth was a mere twenty years after Saint Patrick's passing, and as such Christianity was again in its infancy in Ireland. We believe his spiritual mentor in his early life was a community leader called Erc. Bishop Erc had been a druid in his former pagan life, but after conversion through Patrick's efforts and mission, he became a leader in the tribe and Christian community in Kerry. As such, he took Brendan when he was just a year old to be fostered by Saint Ita in Killeedy, near modern-day Limerick. It is unclear why this occurred—being taken from his family at such a young age to a foster home so far away—but we do know that Ita cared for and raised him as a foster mother, teaching him the basics of the Christian faith on her meager four acres.

Behind every great story lies an unknown mentor who shaped and influenced the key player. Could we be a mentor to someone? If so, we may never know of the influence we may have on a time we cannot yet see!

From Killeedy, Brendan moved around to various schools and Christian communities at the behest of Saint Ita. Brendan clearly had the calling and intellect. He learned Latin and Greek at these schools, which no doubt helped him in later years along with math and science as available in his time. He was clearly a gifted and talented young man; had he not been, he would have ended up working the land or learning a useful trade to help his tribe and community, as most did. Instead, he continued his education all the way through to his twenties, eventually landing at the influential school of Clonard where he was mentored by Saint Finnian, just as Saint Columba had been. Again, in a time when life expectancy was in the mid-thirties, spending your life in schools of learning until your twenties was incredibly rare.

Around the age of 26, Brendan found his way back to Kerry and was ordained there as a priest by his old mentor, Bishop Erc. However, Kerry would not be his final destination. While I suppose the easiest thing the young man could have done would be to take the reins from Bishop Erc and become a leader in his native community and tribe, Brendan was set for adventure...and the call of the sea would be his siren.

> Have you ever felt restless with your lot in life? Perhaps dissatisfaction with a job, or your church, or your friend group? Do you long for adventure but are afraid of the risks involved? Patience and care is needed, and perhaps a mentor's ear—such as Brendan had with Saint Ita or Bishop Erc.

THE LAND OF TIR-NA-NOG

Brendan left Kerry for what would be a life of adventure, travel, and mission. As was true of most Irish people of the time living in coastal communities, Brendan had learned how to sail and fish. He knew how to gather seaweed and identify marine produce. His mentor Erc had also been a druid, so I imagine he may have learned the language of the stars from him as well as how to navigate using the North Star and various constellations as a guide.

I am also intrigued by the thought that Brendan may have learned the pagan myths and legends from Erc, given his past druidic life—especially the ancient Irish myth of '*Tir-na-nOg*,' the legendary land of perpetual youth. We read this fable to our children at bedtime, and its details do have some similarities with the voyage of Saint Brendan.

In the story, the human hero Oisin falls in love with Niamh, a demigod from the otherworld. She brings him to her magical island, called Tir-na-nOg, on a magical horse who travels across the wide sea. There they spend their life together in this land of perpetual youth and beauty. However, after three years, Oisin begins to miss his family in Ireland and begs Niamh to allow him to go back to Ireland once more, just to check in on his kin. She reluctantly grants him his wish and lets him ride the magical white horse back to Ireland, but with one proviso: that he never gets off the horse or touches the ground.

Our hero Oisin makes the promise and rides the magical horse back to the human world across the wide sea. However, he finds to his horror that whilst he has been in paradise for three years in Tir-na-nOg, 300 years have passed in the human world. His family and friends have long since died and been buried. As the story continues, Oisin does end up falling from his horse trying to help an old lady, and as he does, the horse gallops away as he instantly begins to age and turn into a wizened old man who shortly succumbs to aging and dies.

Surely, Brendan would have heard this legend of the island of paradise and youth across the ocean from

Ireland. I sometimes wonder if this legend, when mixed with his Christian beliefs, missionary mind, and inherent wanderlust, played some part in his journey. Perhaps Brendan was influenced to take to his curragh to sea in lieu of a magical horse, sailing across the wide ocean from Ireland…but we will never know.

Restless and Driven: The Navigation

Brendan gathered followers and travelled extensively throughout Ireland, sailing north along the rivers and western coastlines. As I have mentioned elsewhere, in these times it was much easier to travel by boat than by land. He would go on to establish several monasteries and settlements, particularly in Ardfert in his native Kerry and at Clonfert in County Galway, where he seems to have made his primary community. From Galway, it also appears he sailed out to the wonderful Aran Islands and established a community there, and may even have learned from Saint Enda in Aran. From Galway and Aran, he looks to have sailed north along the coast of Ireland and over to Argyll in Scotland. Scraps of evidence and legend tell us he may have established communities in the Hebrides and visited Iona, but it is hard to tell.

The journey for which he is famous, however, was his multi-year journey north to Shetland, then the Faroes, on to Iceland, to Greenland, and possibly Newfoundland and the Americas. This is the infamous *Navigatio Sancti Brendani Abbatis*, to give it its proper title.

The Voyage of Saint Brendan the Abbot is one of the most famous of all early medieval Irish texts and would have been a New York Times bestseller in its day. It is a Hiberno-Latin narrative, probably written in Ireland around the second half of the eighth century, and tells the quite fantastical tale of how Saint Brendan and his shipmates sailed across the ocean, to a fabled land and back again.

The story was clearly written as a fable, not as a serious geographical text. As such, it includes such places as the Island of Sheep, the Island of Birds, a giant cat, a monstrous whale, a pillar of crystal, and fiery lands full of demons. All wonderful in their descriptions, but if we take a step back, many of the places *do* seem to match actual destinations on an Atlantic Sea journey. For example, the description of the strange Island of Paul the Hermit depicts a real place. In the north Atlantic, the islet of Rockall rises from the ocean as an almost circular pillar of stone with steep cliffs and no landing place, exactly as the story describes it. Was this a coincidence, or did Brendan and his crewmates actually observe Rockall in the North Atlantic?

A Modern Recreation

In 1976, the explorer and researcher Tim Severin decided to recreate Brendan's voyage and set about painstakingly building a curragh, that ancient Irish sea-faring boat, using material and techniques from the sixth century. Using this curragh alone, they set sail from Brandon Creek in County Kerry, bound for adventure on the wild Atlantic.

They took no modern shortcuts in trying to recreate what an early medieval Irish seafaring boat may have looked like. It took years to build the boat using tanned ox hides, stitched together with flax cords over a willow frame. The entire hull was then sealed with wool grease (or lanolin, to give it its modern title). Masts of oak were fixed with hand-woven sails.

With a crew and provisions, they sailed north along the Irish Atlantic coast, stopping at Aran and Derry, then onto the Hebrides in Scotland. From the Outer Hebrides, they continued north to the Faroe Islands and then onto Iceland. After waiting out the winter in Iceland, they then began the second half of the epic journey. They crossed from Iceland to Greenland, from Greenland to Newfoundland in Canada, island hopping as they went—all within the confines of an Irish ox hide curragh. In doing so, they proved that such a journey is in fact possible.

Could the Island of Sheep in fact be the Faroe Islands? The pillars of crystal, descriptions of icebergs in the North Atlantic? The fiery demons, volcanic activity in Iceland?

MOTIVATION OR MADNESS?

Brendan may, in fact, have sailed on an epic journey and, in doing so, was a thousand years ahead of Columbus. But even if this is a myth, the fact does remain that Saint Brendan was an adventurer and a pioneer. He traveled extensively and brought the light of Christianity with him everywhere he went. He clearly never forgot the teachings of Saint Ita or Bishop Erc and had a drive and passion to explore and share his beliefs with the wider world, whatever the cost.

One of the hallmarks of Christianity over the centuries has been the incredible lengths its devotees go to in order to spread the word of Jesus and His plan of salvation. While many ancient religions are geographically local and tied to certain cultural communities, Christianity has blown wide the doors of geography and ethnicity. Brave pioneers have taken their message everywhere on the globe.

Crossing the Atlantic in a curragh does sound a little mad, if we're being honest. But with enough motivation, it is quite amazing to think on what we are capable of. The question remains for us to answer: What adventure could we embark on?

In 1996, my wife Judith and I boarded a plane in Dublin and left for America, not knowing what the future might hold. Truthfully, I was a little terrified as I boarded that flight, but I knew in my heart that God would go with us. After all, He had laid the path. He had closed doors in Ireland and opened doors in America. We just needed the courage to walk through them.

Adventure can be thrilling, but it can also be risky and terrifying. You just need to ask yourself whether the risks are worth the eventual rewards. Most of the time, they are. I have spoken to many people who have risked a change of job, a location change, or a church relocation, and almost without exception, they were glad they did. Sure, not every adventure succeeds, but if we are willing to stick out the hard times and trust in God's provision, it can be life-changing and life-giving, not only to us, but to those around us.

God has a plan. Are you willing to ride out the adventure and see where it might lead? Are you willing to leave behind comfort and safety in pursuit of what may be, just as Brendan did?

A Seafaring Prayer from the Western Hebrides

To celebrate the life of Saint Brendan, I will end with a very old prayer, gathered from the Hebridean Isles and written in the Celtic style. A prayer of God's provision in the uncertain world of the journey: the world of the sea.

O Thou who dost dwell in the soaring sky,
On us the tide-mark of glad blessing lie,
Carry us over the crest of the seas,
Carry us to a haven of peace.

Our shipmen bless and our ship fore and aft,
Our anchors bless and blades of our craft,
Each stay, each halyard, each voyaging man,
Keep our tall, stepped masts with their
  mainsails span,
O King of the elements, strong and taut,
That with good success we homeward make port.

My self sitting down in the helmsman seat,
It is God's own Son sets my course complete.

Saint Ita

Simplicity

WHEN MY wife and I emigrated to America many years ago from rural County Armagh, we were immediately struck by the competitive nature and busyness of American urban life. Settling in Atlanta, we were and still are amazed by how seldom people slow down in their lives compared to the slower Irish culture (and yet, the lights remain on in Ireland somehow!)

ALWAYS BUSY, ALWAYS BUSY

People in America are busy, yes, but they are often busy by choice. One Sunday, when listening to a pastor preach a sermon on a completely unrelated topic, he surprised us by declaring that the over-busyness in the lives of Christian people was hurting them and their community. "In the end, we all do what we want to do," he preached. In other words, people are busy because they choose to be busy. It was a startling and refreshing piece of truth.

Imagine for a moment what community and society might look like if people chose to slow down and experience peace and simplicity instead of busyness, complexity, and stress? Imagine if people had room for spontaneity, for the sojourner, for conversation with a stranger. Imagine if they had room for God.

Perhaps it is time to be honest with yourself. The prevailing culture in the United States promotes a strong work ethic, which is good, but also leads to burn out. Can you honestly relate to where you are on this? Are you willing to ask the hard questions regarding your schedule?

The scientific truth is that we as humans are not really that efficient. We like to think we are, but the reality is quite different. We take risks by changing lanes and dodging cars in traffic to shave three minutes off our commute and then spend an hour scrolling on social media when no one is looking, wasting enormous amounts of time. It's hard and very stressful to be super-efficient all the time, which is why I personally suspect God made us both for engaging creative work and for disengaged rest and simplicity. We hate to admit this in our American culture and certainly won't admit it to the casual neighbor when they ask how we are. Much better to state just how terribly busy we are and claim that prize of "productive human."

LONGING FOR SPACE

I distinctly remember a moment many years ago when I watched my first U.S. presidential debate, when George Bush, Sr., for just a quick moment in the debate, looked at his watch and somehow seemed distracted and busy. He *was* the president, after all—I'm sure he had a lot on his mind—but his opponent, Bill Clinton, then Governor of Arkansas, appeared to take time to engage with people in his slow Southern drawl. That moment may have contributed to who lost and who won the election. People were attracted to the person who engaged, who wasn't in a rush, and rejected the person who was distracted and busy. We long for space, peace, simplicity, engagement, and humility, but these commodities are rare. Why is that?

In the early Irish Celtic church movement, a woman appeared who lived a life of stubborn simplicity and quiet, humble engagement. Her legacy remains with us today; she is known as the foster mother of Ireland for how deeply she cared for people, pursuing a humble life in order that she might pour herself into others. She used her ability to enjoy the simple, slow life to influence the lives of people who would go on to greatness. She decreased so that they may increase: the mark of true humility.

When we read the Gospels, it is almost ridiculous how much 'downtime' Jesus employed in His life. He always seemed to crave the lonely places and slow times where He could think and pray. Even when in chaotic situations surrounded by thousands of onlookers, He seemed to have the ability to take time for individuals and be slow enough to be approachable. Traits which are hard for us today in our culture, but all the more valuable for their scarcity.

Saint Ita is one of the lesser-known saints featured in this book, but I suspect she would have wanted it that way. However, I feel her life has some valuable lessons for us today as we struggle with the absurdities of living in the 21st century. Perhaps her way of simple humility might provide a badly-needed pathway for some of us to follow, myself included. Maybe we need to just stop and smell the roses, consider the bigger picture. What would happen if we showed love to the people around us and somehow rid ourselves of the clutter and busyness that keep us from walking a simpler path in humility?

Let's find out.

DEIRDRE OF THE DEISI

Saint Ita, as she would be known, was born around the year 480 AD near a place called Decies-within-Drum, in what is now County Waterford in the southeast of Ireland. She came from the Deisi tribe and appears to have been raised in Christianity. Her parents and family lived just a few years after Patrick's missions, though they lived quite far away from the epicenter of Patrick's life in the north of the island—which shows the remarkable spread of the Christian faith in just a few short years.

Ita was named Deirdre at birth (which is still a common name in Ireland today), and as was the case with Brigid of Kildare, it seems that Deidre of the Deisi had an early affection for God. A distinct calling from childhood, you could say. Her life and Brigid's life overlapped, and we will never know if they met, but Ita has been called the "Brigid of Munster." While there are some similarities in their stories, Saint Ita would not achieve the fame that Brigid did, though this was by design.

As would have been the order of things at that time, when Deirdre came of age her father arranged a marriage for her from within their Deisi tribe. However, Deirdre rejected the offer and appealed to her parents, particularly her mother Necta, to allow her to retain her purity and her singular focus. She wanted to follow the call on her life that she was sensing from God.

At this time in Irish Gaelic society, once a young girl married she moved into a different vocation in life, one focused on her husband and the prospect of having and raising children within the tribal structure. This carried with it a certain honor; we must remember that in the fifth century Ireland, life expectancy was in the mid-thirties. With child mortality at 50 percent, a young woman had to start in her role as a mother early, probably in her teens, and once she did she was fully engaged. Not many considered delaying family matters for career choices back then—there simply wasn't time!

So for Deirdre to reject an offer of marriage was a tough choice and one not taken lightly. It meant denying herself a place in the tribe, which proved to be a tough sell to her father. But in time and with the help of her mother, he came around.

ITA AND HER THIRST

They gave Deirdre the name 'Ita' at this time, which means "thirst," and this nickname does provide us with an insight into her character. She had a thirst for God to go along with her calling; she was going to make her life count.

So Deirdre, now called Ita, set out to start something new. Christianity was still in its infancy in Ireland at the time, so striking out on one's own to build a Christian community and pursue a vocation for a young woman was a very novel idea indeed. It just hadn't been done before; you might say that she was an innovator in this regard.

Ita saw the need around her; she saw the struggles people endured, the orphans, the sick, and the lame, and she wanted to make a difference. She set out with her sister Fiona, and together they found their way to the interior of the island, settling in an area near modern-day Limerick. It was here that she felt a strong call to create a Christian community to serve and help those around her. This was the land of the Ui Conaill clan, from which the modern surname Collins descends. Ita must have made an impression, as the local chieftain of the clan offered her and her sister a large tract of land to build their community, which amazingly Ita *rejected*. Instead, she asked for a mere four acres of land, which she was duly granted, and Ita, Fiona and their early followers set about cultivating this plot of land, building shelters and community together.

As I have mentioned elsewhere in this book, it is important to know that in early Gaelic society the role of women was quite different and more liberal than in contemporary Roman society, which was much more structured. This cultural difference also made its way into Celtic Spirituality which sprang up in Ireland. Thus, societies for women and leadership roles for women were not that uncommon.

Given that most of the interior of Ireland was empty in the fifth century, it does seem strange that Saint Ita only asked for such a small plot. If you have already read the chapter on Saint Brigid of Kildare, by now you must be making mental comparisons. Both women to this point had similar stories. Called at young ages, refused marriage proposals in their teens, and set out to create communities of faithful women. In some ways, it made sense for Ita to have a small plot in a time with no machinery, as it made the land more manageable for the community, but I believe there is more to this. In Saint Brigid's story, when asked to specify the land she wanted, she was granted a massive plot through God's miracle with her ever-growing cloak. Clearly, it seems that God had a large vision in mind for Saint Brigid, whereas in Saint Ita's case, a small plot fitted God's plans.

Most of us have seen large, resource-rich churches with their high arches, vaulted ceilings, and choral choirs. They exude grandeur and majesty, and I enjoy how they reflect the magnificence of God, but I have also been inside many very small churches with simple buildings, small numbers, and a loving community built of neighbors who care deeply about each other. Whilst the former is certainly more obvious and exciting than the latter, they both serve unique purposes. My thought here is that in the grand scheme of things, God does have a plan, and that plan involves both the extravagant and the simple at the same time. Does the small church meeting in a tiny cabin somewhere have less value than the vaulted cathedral? I suspect in God's eyes it does not. What appears to be humble and simple reaches deep into our hearts, and after all, God is in the business of reaching the human heart, not courting fame or celebrity or building extravagant church buildings. Remember, David was a ruddy shepherd boy when he was anointed King, without any trappings of greatness save his love for God.

Saint Brigid was called to great things, even though she walked a path of humility and servitude. Saint Ita was also called to great things, and walked a similar path of humility, but you may have never heard of her before you read this book. Her calling to simplicity and community living was small, but it had a profound effect.

Perhaps you too are called to live life in an obscure way? In our celebrity-obsessed culture, this can be hard to do. But perhaps attending that small living room fellowship is your calling. If so, walk in it.

Saint Ita and her followers created a Christian community based on care for orphans, the poor and the needy on those four acres. They established an orphanage of sorts, the first of its kind in Ireland, and took in many little children, some of whom would go on to great lives after being loved and taught by Ita, including the likes of Saint Brendan.

ANAM CARA

People came to Ita's community from far and wide to seek the counsel of God's humble servant, and as the years progressed the community would be known as "Cille-ida," or Killeedy, which simply means "the Church of Ida, or Ita." The ruins of this community can still be seen today, near Limerick. Saint Ita taught, loved, and cared for those whom God brought to her. She did not travel extensively. She did not seek a larger church building or aim to multiply her ministry into satellite communities. She simply served in a humble way and a faithful manner in the place provided to her and was a soul friend to all who came to her: an *Anam Cara*.

Anam Cara is a phrase that refers to a very close and reliable friend or mentor in the Celtic tradition, with the name being derived from the Irish word *anam*, meaning soul, and *cara*, meaning friend. Saint Ita was an *Anam Cara* to the many people who came to her, providing counsel, prayer, a comforting word, reassurance, healing, and love. Perhaps in this, she serves as a useful measure to gauge our success instead of just productivity and busyness.

It seems to me that we all need an *Anam Cara* in our lives. Is there a relationship in your life like that? Is there someone in your life you can go to when you have hard questions? When you feel downtrodden, beaten up or discouraged? Sometimes a comforting word in season and a listening ear is all we need. It seems that Saint Ita provided that on her humble four acres, free of charge to all who came her way. Perhaps we might follow her example in some way and help someone. Perhaps we can even become someone's *Anam Cara*.

The Celtic term 'Anam Cara' has seen a resurgence lately, and this has led to some confusion with people assuming it is a New Age term. However, it is a Gaelic concept which moved seamlessly into Celtic Christianity, and so I am of the view that we should reclaim the phrase! Be an Anam Cara within your church and community. We all need this, and should reclaim this!

A Prayer of Simplicity and Care

I thought it would be fitting to end this chapter with a prayer of humble simplicity, inspired by Saint Ita. Ita did not leave us any of her own writings, but I am sure she would have encouraged us to make room for God and make room for others and to live simply, humbly, and without pretense.

Father,
We thank you for your generous and
  extravagant love
Which you so freely have given.

With outstretched hands,
May we receive your love today,
May we turn to you today,
May we walk freely in your acceptance
  today.

May we, as estranged strangers
Turn towards You,
Turn towards each other,
Turn towards our stories
With understanding, with listening,
With challenge and change and consolation.

Because we know that you are found
In the spaces in-between.

Amen.

Saint Ciarán

Love

IN THE year 1552, during the last few months of the life of the young Tudor King Edward, a detachment of English soldiers left the garrison at Athlone in County Westmeath, bound for the Irish monastic site of Clonmacnoise. The Protestant Reformation in England had already affected Ireland and devastated the Irish Catholic Church, as King Henry VIII plundered the ecclesiastical riches for his own ends. It seemed Clonmacnoise would be next on the chopping block.

In just a few short months, however, young King Edward would be dead and his older half-sister, Mary, would take the throne in an attempt to restore Catholic authority. But for now, these English soldiers were bent on destruction and pillaging under the authority of the English crown.

What they found was a large campus of sacred buildings that stretched along the banks of the River Shannon. Clonmacnoise was a monastic center of worship and learning, second only to Armagh in its importance, but by the time these soldiers arrived, it had long since passed its glory days. The young soldiers evacuated what monks remained and set about pillaging anything of value that they could find. They burned the buildings and destroyed what they could, and in so doing ended a thousand year-old legacy of Christian endeavor at this beautiful and sacred site. The next five hundred years would see many such acts of wanton destruction in Ireland, but the legacy of this place was cemented in the eyes of millions as it was chosen as the place where Pope John Paul II would hold a Mass for many, amongst the high crosses and beautiful buildings by the river.

Pope John Paul II was the first pontiff to visit Ireland, and in 1979 an astounding 2.5 million people turned out to see him (from a population of 3.4 million). In many ways, the visit was seen as part of the healing process in a country and with a Church that had seen centuries of persecution. Today, Ireland is a radically different country and is mostly secular, as it has increased in confidence, seen great economic success and rejected abuse by the clergy. Interesting, and yet sad how that happens!

Today, Clonmacnoise sits along the banks of the Shannon as a magnificent ruin, but stands proudly in remembrance of an enduring sacred marker. And it all began with a quiet but brilliant young man called Ciarán—a man who loved well.

BOTH BRILLIANT AND BELOVED

Saint Ciarán was born around the year 516 AD to a carpenter from County Antrim in Ulster and a Kerrywoman, who were both outcasts from their native communities and were living close to where Roscommon is in Ireland today. Ciarán's full Gaelic name was Ciarán Mac a tSaoir, which translates to "Ciarán, son of a tradesman or carpenter." The more common Anglicized version of his name is MacIntyre in Scotland and MacAteer in Ireland.

The carpenter and his wife had eight children, all raised in the newfound faith of Christianity, which may go some distance in explaining why they were exiled from their native communities. Remember, Christianity was still a novel and strange religion which was being met with resistance by the Druids at that time.

Saint Ciarán was the outstanding child of the brood, and as was the case with many of the saints in this book, he was noted as being quite brilliant from an early age. So much so that, when still a youth, he was baptized and mentored by a deacon in the area called Justus, who undoubtedly recognized his talent and heart for God and others. Justus raised young Saint Ciarán in the Christian faith, and in time his brilliance led him to be admitted to the famed school of Saint Finnian of Clonard, where he would rub shoulders with other luminaries of the time such as Columba and Brendan.

It's always interesting to me to see how community works to inform, shape, and equip young people. In this time in history, many of these saints would go on to live very harsh lives of solitude, but in their youth, they found their feet and grounding in community. A strong lesson for us today, in a time where people are rejecting church communities, choosing instead to stay home. Isolation might be easy and certainly has less hassle, but inspiration is found in community, where life can be messy.

According to legend, those who knew Saint Ciarán all attested to him being a deep and caring man of love. Columba is reputed to have said of him, "He was a lamp, blazing in the light of wisdom." In time, Saint Ciarán would become a teacher at Clonard himself. I suppose the greatest testimony to his talents lies in the fact that the famed Abbot, Saint Finnian, gave his seat of authority to young Ciarán to occupy when the old teacher traveled. After several years, Saint Finnian even offered Saint Ciarán his position at Clonard permanently. However, there was a wandering bug in Saint Ciarán and he was not yet ready to settle at this time of his life, despite the obvious honor it was to be offered such a lofty position. (Perhaps he had spent too much time with the wanderer Saint Brendan!)

Many tales and legends abound from Saint Ciarán's time at Clonard, all of which point to his loving character. One such story tells of how a fellow student called Ninnidh was desperate after losing a precious manuscript of the Gospel of Matthew. In those days, aspiring monks under Finnian's tutelage were required to memorize entire books of the Bible as they had access to, just as the young Jesus did under his Rabbinic training. With a heart of love toward Ninnidh, Ciarán gave him his own valuable handwritten copy, which meant that Saint Ciarán was not able to commit the entire Gospel to memory. In time, the Abbot came to test the monks. Saint Ciarán failed, as he could not recite half of Matthew, but did not offer up an excuse in order to protect his friend. He wasn't a snitch, in other words.

This incident led to a nickname amongst his bemused fellow students as "*Half-Matthew*,' but on hearing this, the wise old Abbot prophesied, saying, 'Not Ciarán half-Matthew, but Ciarán half-Ireland, for he will have half the country and the rest of us will have the other half." In other words, his love for others may have led to petty shame in this instance, but his love in action would eventually lead to his fame throughout the entire land.

FROM THE ISLANDS TO THE HEARTLAND

Saint Ciarán eventually did leave to seek out the mentorship of Saint Edna of Aran, at the time another great teacher of the faith with great renown in Ireland. The Aran islands are a series of isles off the coast of Galway, which are still a treasure to behold today and have a rich legacy in Ireland. My wife and I bring guests to Aran almost every year, even though they can be challenging to get to, and we just love immersing ourselves in the rich culture of these Gaelic islands. The inhabitants of Aran are all native Irish speakers and we love wandering the island listening to the locals converse in Gaelic, kids chattering in ancient Irish as they walk home from school while old fishermen make jokes in Irish as they work their boats in the harbor.

Aran is full of sacred ruins, including the famed "Seven Churches" and the Dun Aengus fort. An important center of learning a millennia ago, hundreds of saintly students sought out counsel and learning in remote places such as Aran in those times. This is, of course, almost opposite to how it is today, where young people leave rural areas for big city universities, feeling that cosmopolitan life will inform them to a much greater extent. This was never true in the past, where solitude and austerity were sought after, not shunned. Quiet places informed the heart and mind, or so they believed in the Celtic era—so different from our mentality today!

Ciarán spent many years on Aran, learning from Saint Enda on that windswept island. In time, Enda recognized that Ciarán had a calling and advised his most brilliant student to strike out and form a new Christian community in the very heart of Ireland. Note that in early Christian Ireland, most communities of learning and culture were on the edges of the island. On the coast, it was easy to travel by sea, but in the middle of the country with its bogs and forests, the people living there were not so well serviced.

It would seem Saint Enda saw this as where God was calling Ciarán, so he ordained him and sent him out with twelve companions to bring the light of Christ to the very heart of Ireland.

At this point in the story, I must also draw attention to the obvious similarities Ciarán's life bears to that of Jesus. Whilst this might be rooted in reality, it may also be due to some embellishments from the overzealous monks who would write his story some years later. Nevertheless, the parallels are striking. He was the son of a carpenter whose parents were exiles, he was trained in obscurity, and he set out to minister with twelve followers. Nor do the parallels end there, but despite their perhaps questionable authenticity, they are interesting to observe.

Ciarán and his followers left Aran and sailed to the mouth of the mighty Shannon River where they stopped for provisions and encouragement at Scattery Island. Today, Scattery Island is a fascinating dot of an island in the Shannon estuary which can be seen from the ferry if you travel from County Clare to Kerry across the wide river estuary. As I have mentioned many times, in those days highway travel was always by boat, not by land, so islands such as these were important places of provision and living. Another great saint, Senan, actually lived on

Scattery, and records show that Ciarán stayed on this island and with the Christian community there for some time before setting out again to navigate the interior of the island via the Shannon.

THE MEADOW OF NOS

From Scattery, the sacred pioneers traveled upstream along the Shannon before they decided to settle on a superb piece of land that sits on a bend in the river that was called "*Cluain-moccu-Nois*," which means "*the meadow of the race of Nos*," and is known to us as Clonmacnoise. Even today, if you visit Clonmacnoise, it is pretty obvious why they chose this beautiful place. The river bends in a wide arc as it flows through a fertile plain with meadows on either side. I'm sure they immediately saw the potential for farming and settlement.

However, its worth in terms of life-giving provision was matched by its poor defensibility. The meadows by the river are pretty to look at but are easy pickings for raiders. Little did they know that several centuries later, fierce Norsemen would sail that wide river on dragon ships and assault those meadows again and again with devastating results. Grant them this: Saint Ciarán and his friends were lovers of men, not military strategists.

The Vikings, or 'Danes' as they were known at the time, had a catastrophic effect on Ireland, particularly for remote churches and monasteries located near bodies of navigable water. Sometimes I wrestle with God about this, asking Him why He allowed such devastation to occur over such an extended period of time. The Church at the time felt sure this was a judgment from God, but we now know the Danes were just opportunistic raiders interested in silver and gold. In time, they would be absorbed into the Irish culture...but why do you think God allowed such things to happen to good people? Impossible to answer, but interesting to consider.

By now, Saint Ciarán already had a certain amount of fame, and so it was that when they decided to settle on those meadows a young prince of that region came to Ciarán to offer him land and help with its construction. According to legend, that prince was the son of a local chieftain, Diarmuid mac Cearbhaill, who would later become High King of all Ireland; the two are reputed to have driven the first post into the ground together.

Amazingly, we can still view this famous scene today, as the moment was immortalized in stone on one of the panels on the "Cross of the Scriptures," the most famous of the high crosses to be found at Clonmacnoise. The original of the ancient high cross is in the small museum on the site, whilst a superb replica stands in the same place it has for over a millennium. If you ever get the chance to visit, look for the scene depicting Saint Ciarán and the prince on the lower left of the cross shaft. It's incredible to see!

YELLOW FEVER AND SAINT KEVIN

Saint Ciarán soon set about establishing Clonmacnoise with his fellow monks and followers, complete with its rhythms of learning, psalm recital, prayer, charity to the community, and Christian witness. But sadly, within a year of driving that post into the ground, Ciarán would be dead. A yellow fever was sweeping the land which would claim the lives of many, and it seems Saint Ciarán succumbed to the disease at the tender age of 33, according to those documenting his life sometime later. Of course, the age of his death also parallels the life and death of Jesus, and so may be an embellishment.

Perhaps you know of someone who also succumbed to illness at an early age? Or perhaps you have struggled with illness yourself? If so, you are not alone. Multitudes of good people have had their lives cut short, and we can only wrestle with God about this. We will know the true answers when all things are revealed, but in the meantime, it is good to struggle and pray. God is big enough to embrace your feelings and return them with love.

We will never know, but we do know that Saint Ciarán's *Anam Cara*, or soul friend, came to him as he was dying and cared for him in his last few hours. Saint Kevin of Glendalough, who would also achieve much in his own sacred life, ministered to Saint Ciarán and no doubt received inspiration from his loving friend in that small wooden church by the river. In his dying hour, Ciarán gave Saint Kevin the bell from his community, a sign of authority, and in so doing ensured that the legacy he began at Clonmacnoise would spread across the country. Saint Kevin would take that bell to Glendalough in

Wicklow and minister there for the next one hundred years, and the light would continue to burn bright.

For Ciarán, it was a life well-spent, despite being incredibly short—a life spent loving and investing in others, learning from others and building with others. Saint Ciarán did not seek his own comfort, but chose to love loudly, and his legacy very much lives on with us today.

Clonmacnoise is a must-see for any visitor to Ireland with even a remote interest in the sacred history of the Celtic lands. This ancient hub of prayer and learning resonates with an almost tangible sense of the divine. The Celtic people called it and other such sacred centers "thin places," locations where the boundary between Heaven and Earth somehow feels permeable, the eternal just within reach.

Wandering through its weathered ruins, you feel the weight of centuries of devotion. The great round tower stands sentinel, echoing prayers once whispered within its shadow. The iconic high crosses, carved with intricate Biblical scenes, serve as silent sermons, inviting contemplation of the eternal truths they depict. The ruins of the cathedral and the smaller chapels exude a hushed reverence, as if still imbued with the chants of monks who once walked its paths, following in the tradition of Saint Ciarán: a young man who loved deeply and calls on us to do the same.

A Celtic Prayer Inspired by the Life of Saint Ciarán

As a final word, we end with a prayer inspired by Saint Ciarán and all he accomplished.

O God of the river and sky,
Of stone and green hill,
You who breathed life into the quiet earth,
And lit the stars to guide our way,
Be with us as You were with Ciarán,
In the stillness of morning and the shadow
of night.
Bless this ground, O Eternal One,
This place where heaven meets earth,
Where prayers rise like mist from the Shannon,
And Your love flows unceasing as the river's course.
Shield us with the strength of the high cross,
And guide us with the wisdom of the sacred scripts.

Continued on the next page

May our hearts be steadfast as stone towers,
And our souls ever watchful, like the round
tower's eye.
O Shepherd of all, draw near to us now,
As You did to Your servant Ciarán.
May we sow seeds of peace and faith,
And reap the harvest of eternal joy.

Amen.

Saint Kevin

Contemplation

OVER THIRTY years ago, my wife and I decided to take a break in Wicklow. A young couple at the time, we set out from the busy Belfast area and drove down to explore the hills beyond Dublin on a fine October weekend. We were enjoying the peace of Wicklow but had also heard much about Glendalough, the mystical valley with the two lakes. So, being curious, we decided to visit one afternoon. It was wonderful, basking in the autumn light, but we were completely unprepared for the sheer beauty and prestige of the place. There was just something almost ethereal about that beautiful valley between the lakes. The ancient stone buildings, archways, and ruins spoke of long ago, and Saint Kevin's church was a wonder to me.

In many ways, this was the beginning of my journey into Celtic Spirituality. I wanted to know more about the people who built such things. Who had lived here? Why were they here? What did they believe? Surely there was a link between the physical beauty and the spiritual beauty they were reaching for.

It is good to be curious, and I am always amazed how God will sometimes veil His intentions from us in order to prod us along. It's as if He hides and wants us to find Him. It's never obvious at the time, but always interesting how God guides us through choices and curiosity.

DEEP IN THE WICKLOW HILLS

Glendalough is indeed a place of wonder. Among the most intact ancient monastic sites in Ireland, with its ancient churches and almost perfect round tower it sits in a leafy valley between two lakes, hence the name: *Glen* (valley) *da* (of or between) *lough* (lake). Here was the domain of Saint Kevin and his many followers, who lived and loved for centuries amongst the Wicklow hills.

Wicklow lies just south of Dublin and is within reach for most people who visit Ireland, even if only briefly. A day trip there from the city is very easy to do, and if you ever make the journey, you will be rewarded with stunning Irish beauty, as my wife and I were all those years ago. In fact, many people make a special pilgrimage to Glendalough from all parts of the world. The valley, with its steep mountain ridges on either side and quiet lakes, is sheltered from the wind and the elements by the mountains that ring it, giving the place a sense of deep peace. We were definitely seeking some peace in those days as we took a break from troubled Belfast in the early nineties. But truthfully, aren't we all somewhat thirsty for some peace? A place to think and consider our world from a different viewpoint?

Certainly, this was one thought from the founder of Glendalough, Saint Kevin, who not only came to this valley to seek God, but also in time built an entire city here, one of peace and contemplation. A City of God, if you will, in the beautiful Wicklow mountains.

But who was Saint Kevin? What do we know about him?

A QUIET LIFE AMONGST THE BIRDS

Saint Kevin, also known as *Coemgen* in Irish, means "fair-begotten" or "of noble birth." He is an interesting figure. He is very famous as the saint who founded Glendalough, a lover of blackbirds, prayer, and nature.

He is also a bit of a mystery. The annals of his life were written down quite a few generations after he had died and so it can be quite difficult to untangle the legends from the man.

As I have always done as a rule in my research and retelling of these stories, I will lean toward the probable and away from the fantastical. But honestly, some of the stories about Saint Kevin are so good they might be hard to ignore!

Saint Kevin was born to a noble family in Leinster around 498 AD, quite early in the history of the Celtic Church. According to tradition, he was baptized by Saint Cronan and later educated by Saint Petroc of Cornwall, a monk who played a significant role in Kevin's spiritual formation. Cornwall is a Celtic part of Britain, and Cornish is itself a Gaelic language with similarities to Irish. I find it fascinating that this connection crops up here in the story of our Irish saints. I just wonder how much contact existed back then between Ireland and Cornwall. It is a pity it did not continue with more depth, as the Celtic culture in Cornwall has sadly fallen on hard times.

Celtic Spirituality has always been a feature of Christian thought in Ireland, but is lately seeing a resurgence in England, and so it should. Places like Lindisfarne in Northumbria and Cornwall are steeped in Celtic Christian heritage and should be celebrated. In the United States, Celtic Spirituality is celebrated not because of place, so much as family heritage through immigration.

It appears that Saint Petroc was residing in Ireland during these years, and he took Kevin in as a boy and trained him up in the ways of God. Remember, these are the early days of Christianity in pagan Ireland, so perhaps it's not surprising that a Cornish abbot was teaching and leading on the island. There is also some scattered evidence that Saint Petroc may have mentored Saint Ciarán briefly, another interesting connection as these two monks would form an *Anam Cara* bond later in life. Perhaps they met as children under Saint Petroc's tutelage? We may never know.

After many years with Petroc, Kevin underwent more spiritual formation with three reputed holy men in a place called Killnamanagh, which we believe is in modern-day County Wicklow. It was at this time that his deep affinity for nature was noticed and remarked upon. Kevin was comfortable being alone amongst creation; he would seek out places of quiet beauty in order to spend time with God, surrounded by wildlife and scenery, a habit which would become a pattern for Kevin throughout his life.

I should note here that I personally identify with this trait from Saint Kevin. In my youth, I was also deeply drawn to nature and solitude amongst creation, and I believe I found God in those times under trees and by a quiet river in the County Armagh landscape. Shades of Romans 1 come to mind, where Saint Paul reminds us that the evidence for a creator God is all around us if we open our eyes to see it. The book of nature is a testimonial to God, if we would only read it.

THE CAVE AND THE LAKE

In time, Saint Kevin would follow his heart and would seek out somewhere to be alone with God, somewhere that captured the imagination and inspired him.

He found such a place in Glendalough. Legend tells us that after he arrived, he began his solitary existence in a cave by the lake, living off berries and nettles and whatever he could forage. A pretty meager existence, but if you visit Glendalough today, one of the sites of interest that may be pointed out to you is "*Saint Kevin's Bed*," a cave-like opening in the steep rock about thirty or so feet above the lake. This may have been a shelter for him, for sure, or a place of pilgrimage and prayer, but the cave itself is actually a Bronze Age tomb that was carved out of the rock face by people long ago. It is very hard to get to, never mind live in.

Truthfully, it is more likely that Kevin created a shelter for himself and arrived with companions at this place with the intention to create a sacred community. Remember, Christianity in the Celtic tradition is a mix of community and solitude. Most of these early saints embraced both (as should we), build with others, then withdraw to reflect, then build in community again.

A CITY OF GOD

Perhaps Kevin came to Glendalough with the intention of forming a new community. Inspired by his friend Saint Ciarán, he with others practiced life together, building a monastic settlement on the lakeshore. Perhaps they cultivated the land and from time to time withdrew to seek out solitude with the Triune God of creation, as many did in the Celtic tradition. What we do know is that over the course of the next 40 years, this meager settlement would grow into a sacred city with multiple buildings spread across the lower lakeshore. It managed farming, cultivated trade, and housed thousands, creating its own economy. Its reputation grew as a place of learning and community. Saint Kevin's reputation as a holy man grew, and people sought out his counsel and his prayers on many things, including disputes and healing for diseases.

At this time in the sixth century, Ireland was a country without any cities at all. Many cities *did* exist across Europe, such as Rome, Constantinople, and London, as well as farther across the world, in places such as China and Aztec Mexico. But in Ireland, people lived in loose, spread-out rural communities tied together by clans and tribes. Cities such as Dublin and Wexford would only come later as Viking or Scandinavian settlements took hold, so the city that developed at Glendalough was truly groundbreaking in Irish culture. People traveled from all over to visit, and it is remarkable that this city did not develop into a modern town or city as so many others have across Europe.

Sadly, as with other monastic cities, Glendalough suffered terribly during the ninth and tenth centuries from Nordic raiders. It was ransacked and burned many times, and when the Vikings began creating their own permanent cities such as Dublin, Waterford, and Wexford in close proximity, Glendalough just became too vulnerable. In time, its glory days faded, its people moved to safer areas to get away from the Scandinavian warrior raids, and it decayed into the wonderful ruin we find today.

THE BIRD IN THE HAND

But what of Saint Kevin? How did his life develop in Glendalough? As I mentioned earlier in this chapter, historical evidence for the life of Saint Kevin remains sparse, but we do have stories, and it only seems fitting to share two of those stories to end this chapter. Both of these stories were written generations after Kevin's lifetime, and whilst they may be heavily embellished, they also have nuggets of interesting truth. The first story is the most famous, and it involves a blackbird nesting in Kevin's outstretched hand.

This story may remind you of another famous Saint who also loved nature and found solace amongst creation: Saint Francis of Assisi. The comparison may be a good one, as even though Saint Francis was Italian, he was taught and steeped in Celtic Spirituality, deriving from the work of Saint Columbanus in Italy, who we will read about later. As evidence, the famous prayer of Saint Francis is also intensely Celtic in style and rhythm.

Celtic monks from this period of the church valued solitude, as we have seen, and also an aesthetic life that seems overly bleak to us today. They sought hard after God and would deprive themselves of all comfort to do so. They fasted, they exposed themselves to cold and harsh environments, and pushed themselves to the limit, just as Jesus did in the Judean desert, and as the 'Desert Fathers' did, and were an obvious inspiration to the Celtic Christian. Saint Kevin developed the habit of standing in the cold waters of the lake to pray with his arms outstretched in the shape of the cross. Not the most comfortable posture, but that was the point.

One day, as the story goes, as he was praying, a blackbird came and rested on his outstretched hand. Saint Kevin continued to pray, not wishing to disturb the bird, who would go on to build a nest and raise chicks, all as Kevin stood in that cold lake praying. He did not move until the bird flew away, and this story gave rise to the familiar image we have of Saint Kevin today that adorns everything from whiskey bottles to t-shirts and books.

For any of you who may have been to Ireland, you will know that our waters are *cold*. Our lakes and seas are frigid, and standing in a cold lake in a glacial valley would have been deeply unpleasant. But what does this story teach us? The story points to two truths about Saint Kevin. The first is his relentless pursuit of God. He sought solitude and deliberately made himself uncomfortable, all in search of the mystery of God. This seems very strange to our 21st century ears—that someone would seek discomfort instead of comfort—but the Celtic way back then was not for the faint of heart. He may not have truly stood in that lake for weeks as the legend says, but the notion of Saint Kevin depriving himself of comfort and joy, ignoring succor to seek God, does ring true.

The other truth lies in the co-star of the story, namely the blackbird. It does appear that Saint Kevin held a love of the natural world, seeing it as part of creation. In his pursuit of God, perhaps he, as many others have done since, decided that to know the creator, you must know and love the creation...even if the means standing still whilst a blackbird raises her chicks in your palm.

We should honor and sustain the earth God lovingly gave us. After all, He can be found there if we take the time to look—just as Saint Kevin did!

KATHLEEN AND THE NETTLES

The other story is a bit quirky, but also hides an interesting truth about monastic life and intention in this era. As I mentioned before, Kevin's Irish name was "*Coemgen*" which might refer to him being "fair" or handsome, and it seems this did not go unnoticed by the local ladies. The story tells us that one such female admirer came to pursue Saint Kevin at his hermitage in Glendalough. Her name was Kathleen, and apparently she had eyes of pure blue. Kathleen would visit Kevin as he prayed and walked by the lakeshore, making her intentions clear, until one day her advances became too much, and Saint Kevin decided to make a break for it. He ran, chased by the blue-eyed Kathleen, until he grabbed a bunch of stinging nettles and shook them at her. She stopped, and seeing the pointlessness of her pursuit, she relented. Kathleen went on to join the community as a sister, but the story of Kathleen and the nettles remains.

During my childhood in Ireland, I used to dread falling into or running into a bunch of nettles. They grow everywhere in Ireland. They are a weed with spiky leaves that grow in clumps and they sting painfully to the touch. I remember many days when I fell into a bunch of nettles and ran home in tears from the sting, so I can only imagine how poor Kathleen must have felt!

As funny as this story is, it does point to another aesthetic: the chastity displayed by the Celtic saints. These Celtic saints devoted themselves to prayer and knowing God, and it appears they forsook companionship with the opposite sex to fully pursue God with their whole hearts. Of course, this does have Biblical warrant from the apostle Saint Paul which in turn has been carried through to the priesthood of the Catholic Church today. But in the Celtic culture of the time, this was a strange sacrifice. Celtic priests in this era did marry and have families, unlike their Roman counterparts, and familial bonds in Celtic clans were ties of honor, so to deny themselves both carnal pleasures and the privileges of marriage *was* itself sacrificial.

Saint Kevin is reported to have gone on to live a very long and fruitful life, living until 618 AD, so maybe all of that time standing in the old lake water had benefits! So, when you visit Glendalough, as I am sure you will, dip your hand in the lake water and think of this wonderful saint who found God in the beauty that is all around you.

A Prayer Inspired by the Life of Saint Kevin and His Sanctuary in Glendalough

In closing, please reflect on the following prayer inspired by Saint Kevin's life of contemplation in nature.

O Lord of all creation,
Who shaped the mountains and filled the valleys
with streams of life,
Let my soul be as quiet as the still waters of
this glen.
Teach me to dwell in Your presence,
For You alone are my refuge and my joy.
Help me to hold this world with open hands,
As I once held the blackbird's fragile life.
Teach me patience, O God,
That I may tend the work You entrust to me
And care for all Your creatures with a love that
mirrors Yours.

Keep me from pride and ambition,
For You are my only treasure,
And in Your light, I have all I need.
May my days be a hymn of praise to You,
And my nights a vigil of prayer,
Until I behold Your glory face to face.
In the silence of this valley,
Let my heart echo with Your word.
And when my journey is done,
Lead me to the eternal streams of Your mercy,
Where peace and joy never fade.

Amen.

Saint Aidan

Empathy

THE BRITAIN and Ireland of today don't have as many intact ancient holy sites, sacred places, and pilgrimage trails as other European countries, largely due to the religious and political wars that raged on these islands through the Middle Ages and post-Reformation. This is to say nothing about the effects of the Norse raiders we know today as Vikings. Zealous kings, queens, and lords intent on power fought wars that took a heavy toll and left many wonderful sacred buildings in ruin.

However, a few bright spots still remain that draw in pilgrims year after year as they search for meaning and depth in our modern culture. Several of these I have already covered over the course of this little book, such as Iona in western Scotland or Glendalough in Ireland. But one place in particular does stand out as quite unique and unusual, and that would be Lindisfarne.

Lindisfarne, known today as Holy Island, is a tidal island off the coast of Northumbria in northern England. It's almost on the border between Scotland and England, near a city called Berwick-upon-Tweed, and is a special *thin place*, as the Celts would call it.

Thin places in Celtic Spirituality are sacred sites where faithful followers believe the veil between Heaven and Earth is a little thinner than usual. This may be a mountaintop, a holy island, or an ancient church—anywhere people feel they can quiet themselves and hear from God a little easier, just as Jesus did in the wilderness. Many of these places are sites of pilgrimage today, such as Iona or Lindisfarne.

The island can only be reached at low tide when a causeway becomes passable for about six hours at differing times of the day, offering pilgrims and tourists a short window to travel over from the mainland and back. Whilst this might sound very inconvenient to the modern mind, I am actually thankful that the British government has not modernized this island with a bridge to carry traffic. It might seem entirely sensible to do so, especially to our 21st century minds, but it is also a terrible idea. Instead, Lindisfarne remains quirky, special, and isolated in a time of constant connectivity, and I for one am thankful.

This tidal phenomenon between the island and the mainland has existed for millennia, and is one of the reasons why an Irish monk called Aidan chose it as his base for working among the pagan Anglo-Saxons who had colonized the region in the seventh century. The Celtic spiritual mind at the time sought out "*thin places*" that offered both beauty and solitude, and being close to the power structures of men was less important than being close to the power source of Heaven. The latter sometimes requires a special environment to hear its still, small voice. A thin place of prayer, an island that gets cut off by the tide for good parts of the day, fit the bill very nicely.

His Celtic Way

Aidan was an Irish monk living and serving on Iona in the Gaelic kingdom of Dal Riada, which is now Scotland, when he was called to minister at Lindisfarne. Destined to shape the cultures of many, Saint Aidan displayed remarkable courage, wisdom, and gentleness, offering empathy to beggars and kings alike with his embracing Celtic way and spirituality.

I have always admired Saint Aidan and find his story to be so inspirational. How did this humble man find his way from Ireland to Scotland, and then have such an enormous impact on England? Three nations guided by one saint! Thinking about it, if Saint Patrick was an Englishman who ministered to the Irish and became their patron saint, shouldn't Aidan, who was an Irish man who ministered to the English, become the English patron saint? Seems only fair! (I suppose he would need to get past old Saint George and his battle with the mythical dragon first.)

The official patron Saint of England is called Saint George. He was a Roman Christian of Greek descent who was an early Christian martyr, and many countries have adopted him as a patron saint. During the Middle Ages, a fictional story of his battle with a dragon became popular, and it simply stuck, so most imagery of Saint George today depicts him slaying a dragon on horseback.

Amazingly, many people today recreate the pilgrimage that Saint Aidan took from Iona in western Scotland to Lindisfarne in northeastern England, walking those 300 miles in prayer and reflection across the breadth of the island of Britain. This is a tough journey, following a path that crosses mountains, winds through glens, and goes over several bodies of water, but the scenery is incredibly rewarding for those who take up the challenge.

So, what is it about the Celtic Saint Aidan and his journey across Britain that still inspires so many people today? Let's find out.

IN THE STEPS OF SAINT COLMCILLE

Very little information exists about the early life of Saint Aidan. His biographer was a monk called Bede, who is famous in our day as being the first person to write a history of the English people in the English language as it existed at that time, meaning in Anglo-Saxon. Bede was focused intently on the story that was unfolding all around him as the Anglo-Saxon culture developed, and as such, was less interested in Aidan's Irish roots, so we are in the dark a little here. We do know that Aidan was definitely Irish, however, and spoke Irish Gaelic. As a young man, he traveled to serve in the monastery of Iona in the footsteps of Saint Columba and probably came from somewhere in the north of Ireland in the early years of the seventh century.

At the time of Aidan's youth, Iona in western

Scotland was part of the northern Irish kingdom of Dal Riada, which had a common language and culture of Gaelic, so the transition from Ireland to Iona would have been culturally seamless. Founded by Columba some years earlier, Iona was an island monastery in the Inner Hebrides which by now served as a thriving center of learning and worship. It was gaining an admirable reputation, and the greatest minds and most talented students went there to follow in the steps of the great Saint Columba.

No doubt Aidan was a very promising student in Ireland, and so admission to study on Iona was an honor, indeed. Think of it as the ancient equivalent of admission to Harvard or Yale. Unfortunately, things were not going so smoothly in other parts of Britain. As Iona, Dal Riada (Scotland) and Ireland were experiencing enlightenment, England was experiencing turmoil as invading tribes from the continent jostled for dominance.

THE ANGLES, THE SAXONS AND THE ROMANS

After the Roman legions left Britain in the fifth century, its original Celtic peoples (known as Britons) who spoke a language similar to the Welsh language today (P-Celtic) sought to reclaim the land, but

Germanic tribes invading from the east quickly put a stop to that. These Saxons invaded from what is now northern Germany, while another group, the Angles, came from what is now Denmark. Between them, they carved up the land we know as England. In fact, the very name of England is derived from one of those tribes—Angleland.

Fast forward one hundred and fifty years or so and these Germanic tribes were blending into the Anglo-Saxons: a distinct people who spoke a Germanic language that would eventually evolve into English, but who were pagan, whereas the indigenous Celtic peoples had become Christian to a large extent. These ethnic and religious rivalries would sadly but inevitably lead to all kinds of tension on the island. Wars would break out across the land, which would in turn be subdivided into various factions: Celts in the west and north, Angles in the east, and Saxons in the south.

However, these were not the only differences to emerge. Within Christianity itself, a new fault line was appearing. In 597 AD, Pope Gregory sent Augustine to convert the Anglo-Saxons in England, who were growing in dominance. He established a base in Canterbury, southern England, and began ministering and teaching. As he did so, he became aware that another form of established Christianity already existed on the island of Britain, namely Celtic Christianity.

> Celtic Christianity and Celtic Spirituality were meaningful expressions of Christian thought tied with Celtic Bardic culture, but it did not thrive outside of its homelands of Ireland, Scotland, Cornwall and Wales. And so, it was doomed to be dominated by its Roman neighbor. It had a generally peaceful philosophy and did not fight to preserve its place. It was simply absorbed.

As we know, the Celtic form of Christian living differed from the Roman model in several ways. The dating of Easter was a set feast day, not movable; Celtic priests could marry, although most did not; Celtic dress and appearance was quite different, with long mustaches and long hair. They wore mantles, or cloaks and Celtic monks lived and worshipped in a manner similar to the bardic culture around them, all of which would have been a bit shocking to the clean-shaven Romans who adopted the class structure of Roman society into the Church.

In response, Augustine called for a great meeting, or *synod*, and summoned the Celtic bishops to come hither, which they did. They attended the synod but they also summarily rejected Augustine's proposal to join with him as his ecclesiastical subordinates, stating instead that they wanted to stay true to their own people and their own culture, which was something of a rebuke. So, two forms of Christian thought developed side by side in Britain, both Celtic and Roman, which will have a bearing on our story.

OSWALD AND AIDAN

Sometime later, a princess called Ethelburg traveled north from Kent in the south of Britain to marry an Anglo-Saxon prince called Edwin. An arranged marriage between nobles, Ethelburg was a Christian and must have been quite the gal, as she managed to convert her husband and his entire family to Christianity. However, this happy situation would not last. Just two years later, disaster struck when a British pagan chieftain called Cadwallon teamed up with another nasty king called Penda, and together they invaded Northumbria and defeated young King Edwin. They killed or exiled his entire family except for two nephews, who fled to the safety of Iona in Scotland. There on Iona, in relative seclusion and despite being Anglo-Saxon princes, these two young boys were raised in the Celtic and Irish tradition by Celtic monks.

One of these boys was called Oswald. When he came of age, through many maneuvers which would have made a very fine episode of *Game of Thrones*, he managed to raise an army and march against his old enemies, the same men who had defeated his father. Against the odds, he defeated the evil king Cadwallon at a place called "Heavenfield" and reclaimed the throne. It is said that just before the battle, he knelt on the ground before his army and drew a cross in the dirt, rallying his troops.

Oswald then became king in Northumbria, sitting on his father's throne, and he was determined to reclaim all that was lost during his exile. As he was raised a Christian in the Celtic church, when it came to finding help in his mission to convert his people back to Christianity, he did not look to Canterbury in the south, which was Anglo-Saxon and the natural choice, but instead looked to Iona in the north. He chose the Celtic way, which I am sure would have been controversial at the time. It was certainly cross-cultural.

At first, the monastery on Iona responded to this call by sending a monk called Colman, but he failed in his mission and returned after a short period, complaining that the Anglo-Saxons were a barbarous people. On the second attempt, after holding a conference to seek God's guidance, the brothers of Iona chose Aidan, a man full of wisdom, but also one with the right temperament.

He was a person of gentleness and empathy, just what was needed to minister to the pagan English.

Most church plants and missions fail. A crazy thought, but true; it takes real courage to step out of your comfort zone and plant a new church or try to establish a new ministry. I have been involved in several over the years, and they are hard work at the best of times. Looking back, though, they were rewarding. Perhaps you know of a young church struggling to get a foothold in a new place or community. If so, pray for them!

In 635 AD, Saint Aidan set out on his famous journey from the island of Iona with twelve companions bound for Northumbria some 300 miles away, the length of which he walked, as all Celtic monks did. They refused to ride horseback, but preferred the rhythm and humility of walking and meeting people as they went.

LINDISFARNE

Aidan chose the tidal island of Lindisfarne in Northumbria as his base. From there, he could see King Oswald's fortress of Bamburg across the water, while the island itself served as a sanctuary that afforded him and his fellow monks the space and solitude needed to establish their ministry. The Celtic way always puts a strong emphasis on prayer, and prayer needs the right environment.

From Lindisfarne, Aidan embarked on his mission to evangelize the Anglo-Saxon people and convert them from paganism. Unlike his predecessor, Aidan adopted a more patient and relational Celtic approach. He traveled on foot throughout the kingdom, engaging directly with the local population where he could. This humility and willingness to meet people where they were earned him the respect and trust of both the nobility and the common folk. He was overwhelmingly empathetic to the plight and lives of the peasants at a time when overlords sought to dominate, even within the Church.

Aidan's missionary strategy was marked by simplicity, practicality and empathy. He believed in the power of personal example and preferred to teach by living out his faith. He was known for his modest lifestyle, often giving his possessions to the poor and refusing to accumulate wealth, as again would have been true of the Celtic approach. Aidan's humility and selflessness inspired many to embrace Christianity. It was working; this Irishman was winning over the hearts of the English!

Consider for a moment how your approach to others affects your effectiveness. Do you find it easy to empathize and gain the trust of others? It's not easy to do, but getting with people on their level and identifying with the hurts of others without judgment can lead to healing, both of others and of ourselves.

Another one of Aidan's key methods of approach to the pagan people was education. He established schools where young boys, many of whom were freed slaves, could receive both religious and secular instruction. These schools became centers for cultivating future leaders of the Church and society, and Aidan's emphasis on education reflected his belief in the transformative power of knowledge and faith. In fact, there is some evidence that Aidan and his fellow monks would buy young slaves with the specific intent of freeing these children from bondage. It seems they were very much ahead of their time.

As for King Oswald, who had initiated all of this, it seems he was very happy with the person and work of Aidan, and the two worked closely to promote Christianity in Northumbria. Oswald, fluent in both the Irish and Anglo-Saxon languages, often acted as Aidan's interpreter during missionary journeys. This partnership exemplified the harmony between spiritual and temporal leadership in the promotion of the common good. An Irishman and an Englishman working together; if this trend could only have continued, perhaps history may have been different!

AIDAN AMONG THE ENGLISH

Saint Aidan was successful in his mission amongst the Anglo-Saxons due to his Celtic style, his support network on Lindisfarne, where prayer was unending, his calling, and his friendship with the young king.

Oswald seems to have been a good king, perhaps due to Aidan's influence, and he went from strength to strength as he sought to consolidate Northumbrian power, forging alliances and exerting influence over neighboring territories. He is said to have had authority over much of England, possibly assuming the title of *bretwalda*, a term for a dominant Anglo-Saxon ruler. His reign, however, didn't last very long, ending abruptly in 642 AD at the Battle of Maserfield where he was defeated and killed by Penda of Mercia—the same character he had defeated years earlier. According to tradition, Oswald prayed for the souls of his soldiers as he lay dying, which contributed to his veneration as a saint. His body was dismembered and his remains revered as relics.

This was a brutal time in history, for sure. Thrones and power changed hands frequently, but despite all these challenges, Saint Aidan's mission and the Celtic church in northern England gained position and influence, which was amazing in and of itself. In time, several of Saint Aidan's students and followers would gain fame of their own, particularly Saint Cuthbert and Saint Hilda, who are very much revered within the Anglican tradition.

Interesting to note that at this time in British history, the emerging feudal system—which seems quite terrible to us with our modern mindset, and which was brutal with its overlords and violence—was also the cradle for extraordinary growth in the Church. People were desperate for meaning outside the drudgery of their own station and looked to God, to the Church, and to the close clan bonds of their own community for answers. The individualism of our time would have been foreign to them.

Today, Lindisfarne remains a pilgrimage site for thousands who seek solace or prayer on its hills and beaches. Not many of the buildings date back to Saint Aidan's time, having been built over by later Medieval structures, but when you visit this "thin place," you can very much sense the prayers and hopes of those who lived and loved there.

DEMISE OF THE CELTIC CHURCH

In 651 AD, Aidan witnessed the burning of King Oswald's fortress of Bamburgh by Penda of Mercia, who was still wreaking havoc. According to tradition, Saint Aidan then prayed for the flames to extinguish, and his prayers were answered when the winds shifted, sparing the fortress. But soon after, Aidan died at Bamburgh as the battle subsided. He was carried to be buried on Lindisfarne after an extraordinary life of service and influence—a saint for his time, a man of gentleness who won over a nation.

Some years later, King Oswiu assumed the throne and married another Anglo-Saxon princess who, though she was a Christian, had been raised in the Roman style and celebrated Easter on a different date than the Celtic church. The king decided to address this situation and called for a meeting between the Roman and Celtic church leaders at a place called Whitby. For several days they debated, but in the end, the king decided that Northumbria would adopt a Roman style of thought and worship. And so, Colman, Hilda and the Celtic leaders withdrew back to Iona. The center of Christian authority in England would now shift to Canterbury.

This would eventually lead to the demise of the influence of the Celtic Church in Britain, though it would remain strong in Ireland for many more generations. To me, this is quite a sad footnote in history, as the divisions that would later emerge between England and her Celtic neighbors of Scotland, Ireland, and Wales may have been lessened somewhat by a more common culture. We may never know, but it is an interesting thought.

Aidan's legacy, though, continues. This Irish monk who loved his pagan Anglo-Saxon neighbors and won them over with his empathy and the power of the gospel of love shows us the possibilities of transforming hearts and minds for the better. Perhaps we might follow in his ancient path and love others as he loved them, no matter where we find them.

The Prayer of Saint Aidan

To close, let me end with a prayer from Saint Aidan's sanctuary on Lindisfarne.

Leave me alone with God as much as may be.
As the tide draws the water close in upon
  the shore,
Make me an island, set apart, alone with you,
God, holy to you.
Then with the turning of the tide
Prepare me to carry your presence
To the busy world beyond,
The world that rushes in on me
Till the waters come again and fold me back
  to you.

—Aidan of Lindisfarne

Saint Columbanus

Mission

HAVE YOU ever noticed that part of our human condition is a desire for journey and discovery? A longing seems to reside in all of us, one that is prone to take us wandering and exploring, wherever the path may lead. Modern marketers leverage this to sell us all kinds of dream travel products from SUVs to RVs and expensive vacations that few can afford. We delight in the faraway and find excitement in a quest to a distant shore. Of course, there are always the homebodies who prefer to stay within the confines of the family, but I believe it is true that most people yearn for somewhere... somewhere else, just over the rainbow, where the grass is just a little greener.

Certainly, growing up in Ireland and having to deal with its long, cold winters, Irish people have always loved the idea of holidays in the sun and going abroad. My family never really ventured much farther than the north Antrim coast or the Isle of Man, but the dream of the exotic was always very appealing. My mother loved to gather magazines and flip through the travel pictures of all those wonderful, sunny holiday destinations. The coast of Spain, or the south of France; oh, the wonderful time we could have, couldn't we?

The wanderlust amongst humans is strong, but why is that? Why do we long for the unknown and the strange lands beyond the horizon?

IRELAND OF THE NATIONS

In Ireland, there's an old saying that goes: "Being Irish, yearning to leave is like learning to breathe." It's true enough, although these leavings are not always happy farewells. Over the last few centuries, Irish people left Ireland mostly due to war, famine, intolerance and lack of opportunities, but in the era of the Celtic church in the first millennium, yearning to leave takes on an entirely different dimension. Wandering was purpose-driven, other-centered. Irish wandering has a particularly strong legacy, everywhere.

In many ways, Jesus himself was a wanderer at the beginning of His ministry. The distances may not have been huge, but wander He did, and he instilled this pattern of engagement in the early Church. Christians have been wandering for a long time, and Celtic pilgrims were certainly prime examples. We are indeed following in the footsteps of the master.

A phenomenon of our modern world is how Ireland, a small island nation on the edge of Europe, can play such an outsized role on the world stage. Being Irish abroad, we are constantly amazed by this. Here in the United States, the number of Irish-Americans is truly staggering. Up to 32 million Americans claim Irish descent, almost 10 percent of the entire population. Most of the ancestors of today's Irish-American community arrived in the 19th century, following the disaster that was the Irish famine, and spread across the nation from New York and Boston. This only added to the already-existing early wave of immigration that took place in the 18th century before the American Revolution. Most of those early settlers were Scots-Irish folks fleeing religious persecution, who have long since blended into the American mix almost without a trace, save for their surnames in Appalachia. Bluegrass music, clogging, square dancing and whiskey distilling are all evidence of the mark they left on the American cultural landscape.

This is also true in Canada, Australia, England, New Zealand, and beyond. The fact is, Irish people have been leaving Ireland for a very long time, setting up camp in many countries of the world and influencing their cultures in ways that we don't fully appreciate, going back to the first millennium.

WANDERING IRISH MONKS

In the era of the Celtic church, it was understood that there were three types of martyrdom. There was white martyrdom, in which the martyr leaves everything behind for the sake of Christ and travels abroad, never to return. Green martyrdom was when the person deprives themselves of worldly comfort and lives the life of a hermit. Finally, red martyrdom involved the shedding of one's blood for the sake of Christ.

Saint Kevin would have been a green martyr, following in the legacy of the desert fathers, as he lived a life of solitude. We are sadly familiar with those in our world who are red martyrs, following in the footsteps of Saint Stephen. However, we might be less familiar with white martyrdom, and Saint Columbanus very much falls into this esteemed group. He was a missionary, to give him a modern title, who left all he knew for distant lands and strange cultures to spread the news of Jesus Christ. A white martyr, he left family, home and the familiar, never to see Ireland's shores again, following in the footsteps of many Celtic brothers and sisters who also walked this minimalistic path.

Today when we consider martyrdom, we only think of red martyrs. Is this true for you? Consider the potentially chilling effect this might have had on the Church. After all, the ultimate sacrifice is almost too much to bear, but given the choice, many may choose other forms of serving God, if they only understood the cost.

There is a story of three Irish monks who set out from Ireland in a small boat called a coracle, a vessel with no sail and no rudder. They desired white martyrdom and were happy to go wherever God pushed them: no clear direction, just the sea currents and winds of chance; no plan other than belief in God's will. As it happened, they landed on the southern shores of England and were brought before King Alfred of Essex. He was so taken with their story and their incredible faith that he decided to provide shelter and resources for these happy travelers. Thus began their ministry.

These Irish wanderers for Christ were known as "Peregrini," which means *exile*. The desire to leave all for the sake of the mission was called *Peregrinatio pro Christo*, or exiles for Christ, and this type of white martyrdom was distinctive of the Celtic tradition in the first millennium. In many ways, this was an early wave of Irish immigration, but one with a purpose: it laid much of the foundation of Irish influence in the world as we see it today.

THE FIRST EUROPEAN

The influence of Saint Columbanus in the European sphere is enormous. At a time when Europe was still struggling to order itself, a time of feudalism, he and his Irish coworkers and monks brought an aesthetic to the continent that had been missing. Christianity was actually on the decline in Europe at the time, much like it is now.

In many ways, Columbanus was the first true European, coming from Ireland to establish a way of life and order through a community that would have a lasting effect. He converted and inspired thousands and helped to influence law and order with many kings and lords of the time, paying heed to Celtic Christianity. Today, Saint Columbanus is honored in many countries and in many church traditions. There are pilgrimage groups who take inspiration from him; the friends of Columbanus do great work in the church and community and his legacy is very much with us in the 21st century, perhaps more than any other Irish saint outside of Patrick.

But who was he? Why did he choose the path of white martyrdom and leave all? What drove him to be a missionary at a time when such an idea was quite novel? Let's find out.

FROM LEINSTER TO BANGOR

Saint Columbanus was born into a noble family in Leinster in Ireland around the year 543 AD. Over one hundred years after Saint Patrick's time, this region of Ireland southwest of Dublin was now deeply influenced by the Christian monastic tradition that had taken root throughout the land. Even as a young man, Columbanus exhibited a keen intellect and a desire for spiritual growth. He received an education that combined classical learning with Christian doctrine, characteristic of the Irish Celtic schools at the time; he may have even spent time in the company of Saint Snell on the island of Cleenish on Lough Erne. It is said that he was a very handsome young man who would have had many prospects for a successful life at home, but instead he had a calling over his life and left it all for the unknown.

His decision to embrace the monastic life went against the wishes of his family who had likely envisioned a secular career for him, given his talent and good looks, but still he pressed on. A story is told of how his mother begged him to stay after he had announced his intention to leave the family and his community to enroll in a monastery. She apparently lay down across the threshold of the door, quite distraught, but undaunted and determined Columbanus stepped over his mother and sadly bid his family goodbye, never to return. I am sure there were tears that day.

This may seem a little harsh to us in the 21st century, but the resolve demonstrated by the Celtic saints of this period is just one of the markers of their movement. They answered the call of God, deciding on courses that were difficult while leaving family, comfort, and their place in society. Columbanus' resolve was unshaken and he joined the great monastery of Bangor under the guidance of Abbot Comgall.

Does the manner of Columbanus' leaving shock you? I suppose it can be rationalized by recognizing that Saint Columbanus had a strong and distinct calling on his life. Have you ever felt this way? Perhaps you had a strong urge to study abroad or serve in the military, or join a church outside of your family's tradition. Following a calling can be a hard and sometimes lonely task, but one with great rewards.

BANGOR AND BEYOND

The significant monastery of Bangor was founded around the year 555 AD by Saint Comgall (Congal) and would be the place where Columbanus found his ministerial footing and foundation. Bangor means "*pointed arrangement*" and may refer to the pointed sticks that formed a defensive perimeter around the monks' enclosure. There are several "Bangors" in the British Isles and North America, including what is now a large city in Wales. They all trace their names back to the same meaning, although I'm sure the residents of Bangor, Maine have little idea that their city's name means "pointed stick!"

Bangor today is situated in Northern Ireland, just south of Belfast, and is a fairly affluent place with sailboats and golf clubs. But in the first millennium, it was one of the most populated and influential monasteries in Europe. At one point, it grew to house 3,000 of the faithful. Its sacred community and deep aesthetic life drew in many, and in return it sent many out to grow other communities of like-minded Christians under the Bangor rule in the Celtic manner.

The 'Bangor Rule' was a set of lifestyle guidelines that had to be followed in order to become a member of this order and community. Many other orders have similar 'rules' which cover things such as when you wake up, the amount of prayer time observed and when, what you ate, when you ate, and even how much conversation you engaged in. Strict, but strangely harmonious.

Saint Columbanus studied under Comgall and lived for quite a few years at Bangor, learning how to train his mind, body, and heart for the life he would lead. He apparently rose to significance there, but the call of white martyrdom was always on his heart and over his life. And so around the year 590 AD, Columbanus, along with twelve companions, decided to leave Bangor and set their mind on *Peregrinatio pro Christo*: being exiles for Christ.

Bangor is a coastal town, and it would appear that these monks were very familiar with maritime life and sailing, as many in Ireland were. They set out into the wild Irish Sea with few provisions and little forward planning save trust in God. Each monk carried a simple satchel containing a few essential items: a hand-copied Psalter, a wooden staff, and a small wooden cup for the Eucharist. These were their tools of survival, both physical and spiritual, and they knew that God would either take them to where they needed to be, or they would perish on the seas.

The faith of these early Celtic Peregrini is quite astounding. It is difficult for us, living life in the 21st century, to imagine such faith and the actions they took. What would this level of faith look like in our world today? Do we have the courage to set sail with no clear destination, but only trust in God?

They may have made initial landfall in Cornwall, but in time these brave Peregrini landed on the western coast of the Frankish kingdom in what is today France, a land at that time fractured by political intrigue and moral decay. As the group made their way inland, they encountered people who had grown lukewarm in their faith. The once-vibrant Christian communities established by the earlier Church movements were now struggling under the weight of neglect and harsh feudal life, and it was here that Saint Columbanus saw an opportunity for renewal.

THE IRISH IN THE LAND OF THE FRANKS

In the Vosges Mountains, Saint Columbanus and his companions came upon the ruins of an ancient Roman fort at Annegray. It was here that they decided to establish their first community. The monks worked tirelessly to clear the land, rebuild the structures, and cultivate the fields. Their austere lifestyle and deep Celtic Spirituality drew the attention of the local population, who came seeking guidance, healing, and hope from these strange Irish pilgrims.

Annegray soon proved too small to accommodate the growing number of converts and disciples. Saint Columbanus founded additional monasteries at Luxeuil and Fontaine, each governed by his strict monastic rule. His rule emphasized ascetic practices—fasting, manual labor, and relentless prayer, which were familiar to many in the Celtic tradition—but also fostered a spirit of brotherhood and learning. These communities became centers of reform, spreading Columbanus's vision of a disciplined and vibrant Christian life across the region. In a time of chaos, order has great appeal.

Despite his successes, Columbanus's fiery zeal and uncompromising nature often brought him into conflict with the powerful. He openly challenged the Frankish clergy for their laxity and confronted King Theuderic II, the then-French king, over his immoral behavior. The king was living in an adulterous relationship with a woman who was not his wife and wanted Columbanus to bless the sons from this union, even though they were illegitimate. King Theuderic was angry and offended by Columbanus's rebuke, and these confrontations earned him enemies in high places. Queen Brunhilda, Theuderic's formidable grandmother and political advisor, viewed Columbanus as a threat to her influence. Her scheming led to his exile in 610 AD, when he was almost 70 years old.

Queen Brunhilda ordered Columbanus and his Irish pilgrims to be banished and returned to Ireland, and so, under guard, Columbanus and his followers were marched to a ship bound for Ireland. Providence intervened, however, as a three-day storm blew up not long after they set sail. In desperation, the captain threw his cargo overboard to lighten the ship, but the storm battered their sails and destroyed their rudder. The storm calmed, and as it happened, the ship drifted in open water, not back to Ireland, but back to the Frankish (French) coast where they started from. Amazed at this, the captain let the Irish monks go. It seemed that God was not quite done with Columbanus's mission.

It never ceases to amaze me how fearful I can become when it comes to life and mission. I suppose the truth is, if God wants it to happen, it will happen. The trick is trusting despite the storms.

To Italy Beyond the Mountains

Knowing they needed a new path, Columbanus and a small band of loyal followers traveled southward after they landed. The journey was arduous, taking them through rugged terrain and hostile territories, yet these Irish monks remained steadfast, seeing every challenge as a test of faith. Along the way, they continued to preach, convert, and establish small communities of believers amongst the Frankish people they encountered. This journey was years in the making, and in what is now the country of Switzerland, one of the brothers, named Gall, decided to stay and form his own settlement. Saint Gall, as he would be later known, would grow to significance in his own right, and the monastery under Gall would go on to create beautiful Celtic manuscripts, many of which survive today.

Eventually, Columbanus reached the Lombard kingdom in northern Italy, where he found a more favorable reception. King Agilulf and Queen Theodelinda, both sympathetic to his cause, offered him support and protection. With their assistance, Columbanus founded the monastery of Bobbio in 614 AD. Nestled in the Apennine Mountains, Bobbio became his final and perhaps most enduring legacy. The monastery's scriptorium preserved countless classical and Christian texts, ensuring their survival through the tumultuous centuries to come. The Irish were always good at writing and storytelling!

LEGACY IN EUROPE

As Columbanus neared the end of his life, he reflected on the journey that had taken him from the shores of Ireland to the heart of Europe. He had faced exile, hardship, and opposition, yet his mission had borne fruit. His monasteries stood as beacons of faith and learning, and his writings continued to inspire those who sought a deeper relationship with God. On November 23, 615 AD, Columbanus passed away at Bobbio. His disciples carried forward his vision, spreading the flame he had kindled to even greater heights. Today, he is remembered not only as a saint but also as a pioneer who bridged cultures and sowed the seeds of renewal in a fractured world.

It is amazing to me how Columbanus and these Irish monks achieved so much in one lifetime. In an era when travel was difficult, they trekked across an entire continent, over the Alps, and overcame every difficulty thrown their way. Their teaching and reforms greatly influenced the development of European civil law, and in many ways, they helped pull these nations out from darkness and into the light.

Eventually, the rule of Columbanus would be replaced by the rule of Benedict in the communities he founded, but the amazing fact remains that to a great extent, Christian Europe was shaped by the Irish through a very faithful man called Columbanus.

A Prayer Inspired by the Life of Saint Columbanus

Let us end this examination of the life of Saint Columbanus with a prayer inspired by his achievements.

O Lord of all creation,
You who fashioned the heavens with wisdom
And the earth with love,
Guide my wandering heart to the paths of
Your truth.
Let my soul, like the rivers,
Flow ever toward the ocean of Your grace.
May I walk as a stranger in this world,
Seeking not comfort but Your eternal kingdom.
Lord, kindle in me a flame of holy zeal,
To bear witness to Your name among all peoples.
Let the strength of Your Spirit sustain me,
That I may labor without ceasing for Your glory.

Continued on the next page

Grant me a heart purified by penitence,
A mind illumined by Your wisdom,
And a will conformed to Your holy purpose.
May I live as Your pilgrim,
And rest at last in the eternal home
Prepared by Your mercy.

Lord God, cut down and root out
Whatever the Adversary plants in me.
With my sins cleared away
May you sow good sense in my mind,
And goodness in my heart, so that I can seek you
and serve you completely in word and deed,
And understand how to carry out Christ's will.

Grant thoughtfulness, grant love,
Grant purity, grant faith;
Give me all that you know will help my soul.
Lord, work good in me
And provide me with what you know I need.

Amen.

Saint Oliver Plunkett

Reconciliation

IN THE late summer of 1649, one hundred ships loaded with soldiers and siege guns sailed into Dublin harbor over two days. At their head was Oliver Cromwell, the Puritan dictator who had just brought England, Scotland, and Wales under his absolute control, believing he was on a mission from God to do so. He had routed the royalists in England, executed the King, broken the Scots, overwhelmed the Welsh, and now the Irish were next on the block. He had, however, a particular disdain for the Irish, whom he considered brutal rebels and pagans. Eight years earlier, a successful rebellion in Ireland in 1641 had overturned English rule and established a confederacy at Kilkenny. The rebellion was violent, and hundreds of English protestant settlers had been killed. In my home county of Armagh, at Portadown, scores of Protestant settlers were rounded up and drowned in the River Bann at the point of a pike. Cromwell was determined to seek their revenge.

THE HORROR OF CROMWELL

After landing his troops, known as the New Model Army, Cromwell marched north to the walled city of Drogeda (pronounced Drok-e-dah), which sitson the

Boyne River just north of Dublin. They laid siege to the town and, upon entering, gave no quarter. Men, women, and children were slaughtered, and many survivors who had barricaded themselves inside the wooden Saint Peter's Cathedral were burned alive as the roundhead soldiers set it ablaze. From Drogeda, they marched on to Waterford, Wexford, Kilkenny, Limerick, and Galway, burning as they went and killing anyone who stood in their path. Within a year, the entire island had been crushed. Thousands were dead, and Cromwell sailed back to London, satisfied that the Irish had been subdued.

The next 250 years in Ireland would see a period of discrimination and brutality that lives long in the memories of many. However, in this dark time, a light would shine, one whose legacy is still with us today. Oliver Plunkett experienced much of this religious brutality in his life, but instead of revenge and violence, he chose a life of love, forgiveness, and compassion. So, his path is where I would like to end my journey with the Irish saints, as he represents the best of us—the best of the Celtic spirit and the hope that we can rise above it all.

Celtic Spirituality, a belief system that flourished for almost one thousand years in Ireland, was almost extinguished in this period of brutality. However, we do know that Christians have suffered many tribulations over the centuries, which is why Jesus warned us this would happen in Matthew 24. The Irish example is terrible, but it explains why Irish people today have compassion for the marginalized across the world.

IN A TIME OF CONFLICT

It may seem a little out of step to end this book with a saint who was born a full thousand years after the lives of the Celtic Saints whose paths we have walked thus far, but I hope you will indulge me here. I was born in the late 1960s in County Armagh, Northern Ireland, and by accident of my birth, I sadly experienced the worst of the conflict that we called "The Troubles."

It began in Derry, the City of Columba, and engulfed the entire region for decades. I lost a family member and saw terrible things. I experienced hatred and a deep longing for peace. I prayed and worked on reconciliation, as did many, and to our great relief, saw an end to the conflict in 1996 as ceasefires were declared by all combatants, just before we boarded a plane to America.

Those years did mark me, however. The truth is that Ireland is still walking that road to peace and reconciliation. It's an ongoing journey, and whilst we have made great strides, we still have a distance to go as two communities learn to live side by side in the shadow of several centuries of hatred and violence. In 1997, a year after the ceasefires, Saint Oliver Plunkett was made the patron saint for peace and reconciliation in Ireland. A curious decision, some may say, but on closer examination of his life, it makes perfect sense. Saint Oliver lived through the worst of times in Ireland yet saw the best in everyone he encountered. He was and is a light along the very long and dark path from which we are emerging, and as I tell his story here, I hope you will be inspired once more to walk with an Irish saint as we look to a brighter future.

This is his story.

BORN OF NOBILITY AND DESTINED FOR GREATNESS

Oliver Plunkett was born into a family of some means in County Meath in 1625. His mother was related to the Earls of Roscommon, and his paternal family was one of the most respected Anglo-Irish families in the district, the Earls of Fingall. The Plunkett's were a distinguished family by all accounts…except in terms of religion. They were Catholics, and in 17th century Ireland, this came with a price. Harsh laws imposed by the English crown meant that practicing their faith openly was dangerous in these difficult times. Despite this, the family was well-known for their piety and they ensured that young Oliver was raised in a deeply spiritual environment.

From an early age, Oliver displayed a remarkable intellect and a thirst for knowledge. His family recognized his potential early and went out of their way to provide him with the best education, even though they lived in strange circumstances. Initially, Oliver was tutored at home, where he learned Latin, theology, and history; however, the growing restrictions on Catholic education in Ireland forced many distinguished families, including the Plunkett's, to seek opportunities abroad for their young people. So, in 1647, Oliver left Ireland for Rome at the tender age of 22. There, he enrolled at the Irish College, a seminary established to train young Irish priests.

Rome was a city of wonder and learning for young Oliver. He was inspired by the grandeur of its churches and the wisdom of its scholars. Immersing himself in his studies, he quickly gained a reputation for his brilliance and discipline, while his dedication and humility earned him the respect of his peers and mentors alike. It was clear to all that this young man was something special.

A common theme that has popped up in the stories of several of our Irish saints has been the effect of directed spiritual guidance when these exceptional people were in their youth. It makes me wonder if we should consider this as something to invest in in our lives. My wife and I volunteered to teach youth for eight years at our church, and we were glad we did. We invested in the future. How are you investing?

The years Oliver spent in Rome were transformative. He not only deepened his theological knowledge but also developed a broader understanding of the challenges facing the church in Ireland, and perhaps in his mind, how to revive it. Despite being far from home, Oliver's thoughts very much remained with the suffering people of Ireland during these years, and he resolved to dedicate his life to their service, even if it meant his death.

In 1654, Oliver was ordained a priest, marking the culmination of years of study and spiritual preparation. Normally, this would be the time when a seminarian would return to his home country, but as Ireland was still suffering under Cromwell's sword, he remained in Rome for several more years serving as a professor of theology and canon law. He bided his time. He prayed, he fasted, he taught, and he waited.

A RETURN TO IRELAND

The news from Ireland was bleak. The country had suffered greatly from war. Towns, farms, and villages had been devastated. Catholic priests and bishops were being actively hunted down and executed, incredible as that may seem to us today. The very heart was being ripped out from the close-knit Irish communities that normally revolved around their local church, as they had done for a thousand years. Oliver Cromwell, now the Lord Protector of the Commonwealth, died in 1658, but the persecution in Ireland did not stop with his demise, even after the monarchy was restored in

England. The young Charles Stuart, eldest son of the executed Charles I, was invited to retake the throne and return from exile in France, where his family had been living under the protection of the French King. This ended a wretched decade of puritan rule in England, which had been austere and repressive, but young prince, now crowned as Charles II, played his religious cards very carefully. His wife was Catholic, and he himself was a closet Catholic, but the Protestant fervor in England demanded a Protestant King, and Charles played the part very well. It *was* good to be king, after all.

By 1670, the situation in Ireland had become catastrophic. The last three Catholic bishops active on the island had been captured and executed, and the elderly Archbishop Talbot was ill and close to death. The Church was near to complete collapse. Pope Clement IX had to come up with a plan to revive the church in Ireland, and when given the options, he declared, "Why should we look about when the best choice is right before our eyes in Rome!" And with that, he chose Oliver Plunkett to be the Archbishop of Armagh and of Ireland, making him the successor of Saint Patrick.

And so it was that Oliver Plunkett set out to return to Ireland.

CAPTAIN BROWN AND THE UNDERGROUND CHURCH

Given the prejudices towards Rome, it was decided that Oliver should travel first to Ghent in Belgium, then travel from Belgium to Britain, thus raising fewer suspicions. In the spring of 1670, under a veil of secrecy, he traveled with a small party to London from Belgium and was received discreetly by the Queen, who was a Catholic, as you may recall. After several weeks being briefed on the situation in England and Ireland, still under the protection of the Queen, Oliver made his way north and again in secrecy, over the sea to Ireland once more.

I'm sure there were tears in his eyes as he landed on Ireland's shores after 25 years of self-imposed exile, but God clearly had a plan for this man. And, like many of the great characters whom God chooses, they are always tested and trained before their ministry. And a good thing, too, as Oliver Plunkett would be tested again…with fire.

There is an interesting parallel here to the many examples of Biblical heroes who suffered exile and wilderness experiences before God used them: Moses in the Midian desert, Joseph rotting in an Egyptian prison on trumped-up charges; David herding sheep and wasting time in the hills. Even Christ Jesus himself in the bleak wilderness after His baptism fits the bill. Maybe your own desert experiences aren't in vain?

After arriving in Armagh in utter secrecy, Archbishop Plunkett set about trying to heal the vast wounds around him and bring some sort of organization back into a devastated and discouraged church and its people. For the first few months, he traveled under a pseudonym of "Captain Brown," complete with a wig, pistol, and sword. Despite this, God *did* open doors for him. He saw to the ordination of scores of new clergy and confirmed thousands of new converts, all in secrecy. He lived in safe houses, slept in barns, and lived rough in the woods and fields. The priest hunters were everywhere, and ransoms were paid to turn in anyone of suspicion. It was a dangerous time, but like so many other times and places in the world where Christians suffer persecution, the Church still grew. What makes this period of Irish history particularly sad, however, is the fact that these Christians were being persecuted by other Christians, all in the name of God.

Oliver's ministry grew, and as the years wore on, he emerged from secrecy whilst still keeping a careful eye on his company and surroundings. He reached out to his Protestant counterparts and began to form relationships with the Anglican bishops and some of the English aristocracy who were ruling the country. This even developed to a stage where the English Viceroy, Lord Berkeley, asked for his help in subduing the violence that was happening with the Tory rebels.

At that time, Irish rebels who had formed of bands of resistance fighters, were roaming the country, living in the woods and on islands. These rebels were nicknamed "Tories" and they raided and burned settlers' farms and towns in reprisal for the English settlements that had taken Irish land. Oliver agreed to help end the violence and arranged a meeting with fifteen of the rebel Tory leaders, all of whom were condemned men. He managed to get them to agree to end their violence, and in return, they could have safe passage to the continent whilst their fighters could return to their homes and farms without penalty. It worked, and the Tory rebellion subsided, but many in the native Irish community did not agree with

Oliver's peacemaking, seeing it as bowing to English pressure.

Despite this, Oliver's work in the community was bearing fruit. The wounds of conflict were beginning to heal. Injustice was everywhere, but Saint Oliver never walked a path of revenge; only peace, seeing the only possible future being life together.

THE POPISH PLOT

The religious fervor of this time might seem strange from a 21st century perspective, especially when we live in a Western world where the concept of secularism is the mainstream. But in the 17th century, religious views were held very passionately—passions that were a powder keg that was easily exploited and exploded.

Into this maelstrom came a very unsavory character who would light the fuse on this powder keg. His name was Titus Oates, a discredited individual who had been expelled from several educational institutions and had been marked by scandal, namely theft and cheating. In 1678, Oates and his associate Israel Tonge concocted the story of the Popish Plot, claiming that Catholic leaders were planning to assassinate King Charles II and install his Catholic brother James, the Duke of York, on the throne. Oates alleged that Jesuits and other Catholic figures were central to this conspiracy, presenting forged documents and false testimonies to support his claims.

Oates's accusations ignited a wave of anti-Catholic hysteria across England. Dozens of innocent Catholics were arrested, and many were executed based on Oates's perjured testimony. The government, eager to capitalize on the public's fear of Catholics, supported Oates and used the fabricated plot as a pretext to suppress Catholicism further. This hysteria led to the spotlight falling on Archbishop Oliver Plunkett in Ireland, and in the course of time, he was arrested by the authorities on the vaguest of charges and held in Dublin Castle. He was denied the right to hear of his charge, and over the space of a year, the entire arrest and accusation drama became what can only be described as a farce. When the authorities tried to bring two witnesses in to testify against Oliver, one absconded, and the other showed up drunk, so they were left with no alternative but to release him.

TO LONDON AND THE LION'S DEN

Lord Shaftesbury, a leading politician in England who was blatantly using the hysteria against Catholics for his own means, desperately wanted to land the arrest and trial of Archbishop Oliver Plunkett. He knew well that the trial of the leading Irish Catholic would be popular amongst England's Protestants and would serve his own cause and career. So, Shaftesbury had troops track down Archbishop Plunkett, who was duly arrested and shipped to England and held in a filthy prison with the lowest of criminals to await a trial. As before, he was denied the right to know the charge over which he had been arrested, and when eventually presented with the date of his trial, he was only given a few weeks to stage a defense. However, with communication impossible, as he was being held in an English prison, he had little support.

According to Open Doors International, a non-profit organization that tracks persecution and injustice around the world, 4,744 Christians have been arrested and imprisoned for their faith this year alone. The accurate figure is likely to be significantly higher, as many of the countries where gross injustices happen are closed nations that strictly control journalism. Perhaps consider praying for or giving something to help the plight of those suffering injustice, just as Saint Oliver did.

The arrest and proposed trial had by now gained significant public interest in London. It was to be a show trial, if you will, and while Oliver was not allowed any defense counsel, the crafty Lord Shaftesbury had lined up no fewer than nine witnesses against him, each one coached with a story and each on the payroll of Shaftesbury himself.

The trial began in June 1681 when interest was at a fever pitch. The Lord Chief Justice Sir Francis Pemberton would preside, and a strongly biased jury was selected. Archbishop Plunkett was accused of plotting to overthrow the King, conspiring with French and Spanish forces, and high treason. Witness after witness, most of whom were apostate priests and criminals, told very high tales of Saint Oliver's exploits, none of which had any bearing in reality. But in England, with an all Protestant jury, the incredible nature of these testimonies was simply overlooked. Saint Oliver pled his innocence but was chastised several times by the Chief Justice and denied even the barest hint of due process.

In the end, after a farcical procedure, the prosecution rested. The jury deliberated, and in a mere fifteen minutes, they reached a unanimous verdict of guilty. Archbishop Oliver Plunkett, a man who had lived for peace and justice, stood condemned. On hearing the verdict, Plunkett remarked, "*Deo gracias*," meaning, 'God be thanked.'

Deo gracias or *gratias* is a common expression used in the Roman Catholic liturgy, particularly as a response after readings and at the end of Mass. It signifies gratitude to God for blessings received, and while it is open to interpretation why Saint Oliver used this phrase when the verdict was handed down, it is my belief that he considered the fact that he was chosen to suffer the injustice of a show trial, as Christ did, a privilege. And so, he gave thanks for the great honor.

A TERRIBLE DEATH

Just 17 days later, Oliver Plunkett, the Archbishop of Ireland, was taken from Newgate prison, tied to a wooden hurdle, and dragged through the London streets to his place of execution at Tyburn. Here, he was hanged, drawn, and quartered. As the hangman knotted the rope around his neck, he spoke to forgive his accusers, all of those who wished him harm, and even the executioner. As the noose was drawn tight, he repeated reverently, "Into Thy hands, O Lord, I commend my spirit. Lord Jesus, receive my soul." In so doing, he reenacted the words that Jesus spoke on the cross as He finally succumbed to the Roman execution. No doubt, Saint Oliver had that scene on his mind as he faced his final moments.

Following his undignified public hanging and in a final act of brutality, his head was severed and placed on a spike, while his bodily remains were dispersed, or else quartered and buried separately.

The very next day, the "Popish plot" collapsed and Titus Oates, along with Lord Shaftesbury, were arrested and imprisoned by the King, who clearly understood the travesty which had taken place. Several of the witnesses confessed to their lies and begged forgiveness, but the damage had been done. Saint Oliver Plunkett was dead. He would be the very last Catholic martyr to die in England and one of the last people to die in such a public execution.

Oliver Plunkett's head was retrieved and smuggled to Ireland, where he was given a burial of sorts with all the honors due his office. After the ceremony, his head was transported to Armagh and eventually to a place of honor in the newly reconstructed Saint Peter's Church in Drogheda—the very same place where, during the Cromwellian war a generation earlier, many innocent souls had been burned alive. His head is still in that church today, and there he rests.

LEGACY

Oliver Plunkett was canonized in 1975, becoming the first new Irish saint in almost seven hundred years and linking him with the wonderful saints whose paths we have discussed thus far. To me, he remains perhaps the most consequential of the Celtic Saints. Oliver Plunkett's life, arrest, trial, and execution spanned the worst of ethnic and religious intolerance, but the question remains whether we can rise above this. Hatred is easily spread, rumors can easily infect and fester, while forgiveness and peace-making are difficult at best.

Consider the consequences of love and forgiveness in your own life. In light of such an example, what can we do to love others and pray for those who wrong us, as Jesus taught us to pray? There will always be injustice. There will always be those who mean us ill. Can we choose love in response, as Saint Oliver did?

In May 2011, Queen Elizabeth II visited Ireland at the request of Mary McAleese, the then-Irish president. The visit was a monumental moment in Anglo-Irish relations and an opportunity to deepen the peace between their nations. At a state banquet held in her honor, she opened her speech with introductory words in Gaelic Irish, and spoke of the hurts of the past and the desire for peace and change. The Irish president and everyone else who watched the speech were stunned. The fact that a British monarch could reach out with empathy in Ireland was groundbreaking and deeply healing. Since then, many leading figures have offered apologies and sought forgiveness for the wrongs of the past from both sides of the divide. Saint Oliver, no doubt, would be smiling on such things as we try to leave the hurts of the past behind and seek a brighter future.

So, as we look back at the long road of Irish history, one cluttered with tragedy, the life of Saint Oliver Plunkett stands out as a peace maker in a time of war. He carried a heavy burden through his life, but perhaps he did so in order that we could live free.

And so we shall, with God's help. Joy on the journey!

A Prayer for Peace Inspired by the Life of Saint Oliver Plunkett

Dedicated to the thousands who lost their lives during the Troubles in Northern Ireland, and indeed throughout the world due to violence and intolerance. A better day is coming soon.

O High King of Heaven,
Bearer of light, Bringer of peace,
Let Your grace fall like gentle rain
Upon this weary world.
By the wisdom of the ancients,
By the strength of the earth,
By the rhythm of sea and sky,
May harmony be restored.
Let the winds carry away all strife,
Let the rivers wash away all sorrow,
Let the fire of love burn bright in every heart,
And let the land rest in Your peace.

Continued on the next page

Lead me from death to life, from falsehood
to truth.
Lead me from despair to hope, from fear
to trust.
Lead me from hate to love, from war to peace.
Let peace fill our hearts, our world, our
universe.

Peace. Peace. Peace.

Closing Remarks

I do hope you have enjoyed—and perhaps even been inspired by—this journey through the lives and virtues of these Irish saints, whose lives spanned 1,200 years from Patrick to Plunkett. It is a strange irony that God granted such favor to Celtic Spirituality for a thousand years, allowing these virtues to flourish, but then allowed the nation to be plunged into centuries of war, famine, and intolerance. Difficult to understand from our perspective, but then again, we must remember that the lives of the righteous and the virtues they display will have consequences in the real world. We become a target for a spiritual evil that seeks chaos in the world. Jesus said that troubles would find those who followed His example, and unfortunately, time has borne this out. But we should take heart, as He has overcome the world!

Righteous virtues are hard to live out, if we are being honest with ourselves. But a life of virtue is always worth the challenge, in my view, and it is good to reflect on the lives of the godly saints who have exemplified these virtues in their lives despite their enormous cost.

Without courage, Saint Patrick would have remained on that windy hillside herding sheep, and the 17th of March would just be another day in our calendar. Without her nurturing love and the simplicity of those four humble acres, Saint Ita would be forgotten, and many of the subsequent saints in this story would never have arisen. Without Aidan's enduring empathy and compassion, the early English Anglo-Saxons may never have heard the gospel or been introduced to Christian ethics as early as they were, which would have had a profound effect on history. Without the missions and work of Saint Columbanus, Europe might not have been exposed to Christian ethics and may not have injected these virtues into its prevailing laws and social morals as those countries emerged into the Medieval era. Without the forgiveness and heart of reconciliation displayed by Saint Oliver, we may not have had a blueprint to follow when striving to seek peace, as Christians have done now for centuries.

So, did they make a difference by displaying and living such virtues? Yes, they did! And the good news is that we can also strive to live virtuous lives, which can only bring good into the world around us. As I've said before, there will always be haters and people who are narrow and bitter in their lives for various reasons, but we can be the engine of change. We can make a difference if we decide to, and follow the saints' example.

I hope that you have caught a glimpse of the culture of Celtic Spirituality and of that unique calling that God seems to have given to the Irish people. There are many books out there displaying various aspects of Celtic

Spirituality, many of which are helpful and insightful. But for my part, in my closing comments here, I appeal to you, dear reader, to perhaps visit the island of Ireland and get to know the Celtic spiritual culture for yourself.

Maybe visit Clonmacnoise or Glendalough and walk among the high crosses carved with such skill and devotion over a thousand years ago. Gaze out at an Atlantic sunset or climb a mountain before lunch, or dip your toes in a cold Irish lake and think of Saint Kevin. Visit Saint Patrick's grave in Downpatrick or sail over the Irish Sea to Iona and experience that green jewel of an island, sitting tranquil in a turquoise sea. See for yourself and be inspired by the Celtic heart. Take time out to read some poetry from the Celtic lands or listen to some music. The Christian heritage from the Celtic lands, which we call Celtic Spirituality, has a wonderful richness waiting to be discovered and I can only hope this little book has given you a taste.

So if I may, let me close with a final Celtic-inspired poem which pays tribute to these wonderful saints and the land from which they came.

—Gary McLoughlin

Of Ireland and Her Saints

A mist hangs low in the valley
As the birdsong begins.
The wood pigeon and cawing crows
Announce another day of green hedgerow haven
    and stonewall sanctuary in Erin's green land.

Ancient feet trod these fields
Long ago,
And forged paths
That led the way
For all of us to follow
And find.

As the mountains rise
And spill out the rivers that
Run through the peat bog lows
Of hawthorn and oak
They whisper in the wind,
Of virtues that I long to catch and hold.

To stand with courage,
To love with compassion,
To give, and not to count the cost.

A simple bell rings
And we recall those who loved without borders
Dreamt of a better day
And called us all home once more.

Our saints for our sinners
And a life worth living
On this wind swept island
At the edge of the world.

Ireland.

About the Author

Gary McLoughlin is an artist, designer, writer, musician and worship director who loves culture, history and sacred devotion. He grew up in County Armagh in the North of Ireland and emigrated to the United States in 1996, settling in Atlanta, Georgia where he and his wife established a food and travel company called The Shamrock and Peach.

Together, they spend months out of the year showcasing the beauty and culture of Ireland on their various tours of the Emerald Isle. Gary has also led worship in several churches over 30 years, both in Ireland and in the United States, and has a deep love for sharing sacred songs, liturgy and poetry. He has long held a passion for Celtic Spirituality, a belief system rooted in the history and stories of his homeland.

For more information, visit:
www.theirishsaints.com
www.shamrockandpeach.com

Bibliography

David Adam, *The Cry of the Deer.* Holy Trinity Church, 1987.

David Adam, *The Edge of Glory.* Triangle Books, 1985.

David Adam, *The Rhythm of Life.* Holy Trinity Church, 1996.

David Adam, *A Desert in the Ocean.* Triangle Books, 2000.

Tracy Blazer, *Thin Places.* Leafwood Publishers, 2007.

Thomas Cahill, *How the Irish Saved Civilization.* Nan A. Talese, 1995.

Gabriel Cooper Rochelle, *A Staff to the Pilgrim.* Golden Alley Press, 2016.

Tom Davies, *The Celtic Heart.* Triangle Books, 1997.

Joseph Duffy, *Patrick in His Own Words.* Veritas Publications, 2019.

Stella Durand, *Dove of the White Flame.* Resource Publications, 2020.

Stella Durand, *Through the Year with the Irish Saints.* Veritas Publications, 2020.

Mary C. Earl, *Praying with the Celtic Saints.* St. Mary's Press, 2000.

Antonia Fraser, *Cromwell.* Grove Press, 1973.

Ian Bradley, *The Celtic Way.* Darton, Longman and Todd Ltd., 1993.

Ian Bradley, *Following the Celtic Way.* Darton, Longman and Todd Ltd., 2018.

Timothy Joyce, *Celtic Christianity.* Orbis Books, 1998.

Colm Lennon, *The Incomplete Conquest.* Gill & Macmillan, 1994.

Brian Mac Cuarta SJ, *Ulster 1641.* W & G Baird Ltd., 1993.

G.R.D. McLean, *Praying with the Celts.* Triangle Books, 1998.

Calvin Miller, *The Path of Celtic Prayer.* InterVarsity Press, 2007.

Michael Mitton, *Restoring the Woven Cord.* Darton, Longman and Todd Ltd., 2018 (2024).

Alistair Moffat, *The Sea Kingdoms.* Harper Collins, 2008.

John O'Donohue, *Anam Cara.* Harper Collins, 1997.

John O Riordain, *Early Irish Saints.* The Columba Press, 2001.

Elizabeth Rees, *Celtic Saints of Ireland.* The History Press, 2013.

Elizabeth Rees, *Celtic Saints: Passionate Wanderers.* Thames & Hudson, 2000.

Robert Reilly, *Irish Saints.* Wings Books, 1964.

Hilary Richardson & John Scarry, *An Introduction to Irish High Crosses.* Mercier Press, 1990.

Katherine Holman, *The Northern Conquest.* Signal Books Ltd., 2007.

Kevin Vost, *Three Irish Saints.* TAN Books, 2012.

Like this book?
Take a look.